PRODUCTION LINE TO FRONTLINE

LOCKHEED
P-38
LIGHTNING

SERIES EDITOR: TONY HOLMES

PRODUCTION LINE TO FRONTLINE • 3

LOCKHEED

P-38 LIGHTNING

Michael O'Leary

OSPREY
AVIATION

FRONT COVER Exceptionally clear view of P-38J-10-LO USAAF s/n 42-68008 on a test flight near the factory during late 1943. This was one of the first non-camouflaged Lightnings built by Lockheed

BACK COVER Lockheed Chief Engineering Test Pilot Milo Burcham poses in front of 'his' Lightning at Burbank, clutching his flight bag. Nicknamed *YIPPEE*, and given a special overall-red paint scheme, this P-38J-20-LO was the 5000th Lightning built by Lockheed

TITLE PAGE A Lockheed worker checks the breech mechanism of a .50 cal air-cooled Browning machine gun installed in the nose of a P-38E. This view gives a good idea of the Lightning's concentrated firepower, and shows the extra panel installed for the 20 mm cannon

First published in Great Britain in 1999 by Osprey Publishing
Elms Court, Chapel Way, Botley, Oxford, OX2 9LP

ISBN 1 85532 749 X

Edited by Tony Holmes
Design by Gwyn Lewis
Cutaway Drawing by Mike Badrocke
Scale Drawings by Mark Styling

Origination by Valhaven Ltd, Isleworth, UK
Printed through Worldprint Ltd, Hong Kong

99 00 01 02 03   10 9 8 7 6 5 4 3 2 1

EDITOR'S NOTE
To make this series as authoritative as possible, the editor would be extremely interested in hearing from any individual who may have relevant photographs, documentation or first-hand experiences relating to the elite pilots, and their aircraft, of the various theatres of war. Any material used will be fully credited to its original source. Please write to Tony Holmes at 10 Prospect Road, Sevenoaks, Kent, TN13 3UA, Great Britain.

FOR A FREE CATALOGUE OF ALL BOOKS PUBLISHED BY OSPREY PLEASE WRITE TO:
The Marketing Manager, Osprey Publishing Limited, PO Box 140,
Wellingborough, Northants, NN8 4ZA

CONTENTS

INTRODUCTION

WELCOME TO THE THIRD VOLUME in Osprey's *Production Line to Frontline* series. As with previous books, we have attempted to place the Lockheed P-38 Lightning in its original environment – from the design of the prototype to the conclusion of World War 2. And once again, the reader will not find any restored warbirds within the covers of this tome – rather, we have relied on period photographs in the attempt to define a very unique, and short, period in American history. Reeling from the effects of the Great Depression, American aeronautical firms were just starting to recover during the late 1930s with massive orders from foreign governments suddenly made aware of the dangers of Nazi Germany.

Lockheed was one such aircraft builder. Located in the then bucolic community of Burbank, California, the company had attained fame with its wooden series of record-breaking aircraft that included the Vega and Orion. When the brief age of all-wood aircraft came to an end, Lockheed boldly entered into the world of all-metal transports, producing such revolutionary designs that included the Model 10 and Model 12. However, the company's financial state was always rather 'touch-and-go', as they relied mainly on civil contracts – the more lucrative, but limited, military contracts usually eluded the firm. Although the company was small, it was extremely creative, with Hall Hibbard and the young 'Kelly' Johnson casting their creative visions into the future, and replying to a military specification with an aircraft that would carve history in the strife-filled skies of the 1940s – the Lockheed XP-38.

The history of the P-38 is filled with numerous engineering and aerodynamic problems, for the company built an aircraft to go where no others had previously gone – high altitudes at high speeds. The fact that the majority of these problems were successfully rectified is a tribute to the men and women of Lockheed, and early variants of the P-38 were meeting and defeating the Japanese Empire within months of the disastrous Pearl Harbor attack in December 1941.

Lockheed grew at a rate totally unexpected by management, the company hiring up to 500 people a day, buying hundreds of acres of land (including the Union Air Terminal, which became the Lockheed Air Terminal), and constructing huge new buildings to house the production of a variety of combat aircraft. Readers interested in the subject should try to find a copy of the film *Wings for the Eagle* (made by Warner Brothers in 1941, and starring Ann Sheridan and Dennis Morgan), for it details – albeit in dramatic form – the rapid growth of Lockheed immediately prior to, and after, America's entry into World War 2. There are some wonderful scenes of Hudson and early P-38 production, along with the sense of urgency and enthusiasm that permeated the period.

Aside from becoming a successful combat aircraft in the fighter, bombing, and reconnaissance roles, the P-38 also became something of a social icon. Since its shape was so immediately identifiable, the aircraft was lauded in song and, oddly, in jewellery, with its distinctive shape being reproduced in Lucite pins and gold earrings, along with many other items.

Today, the P-38 remains one of World War 2's most revered surviving aircraft – only a half-dozen still take to the air as we near the end of the 20th century. However, the aircraft is still one of the most recognised, and admired, by the general public at any air display.

Numerous photographs in this volume are courtesy of Lockheed, and I must thank friends Denney Lombard and Eric Schulzinger for helping me sift through the maze of stored files and photographs buried within the Lockheed Martin Corporation structure. However, sitting in a warm office going through historical P-38 documents was a bit more pleasant, in the physical sense at least, than some of the dark and cold nights we spent recording SR-71 Blackbird operations in remote locales. Thanks also to Scott Bloom for once again making his large file of vintage advertisements available. These ads, along with the photographs, help define the time period – one that is not far removed in years, but seems to have been lost forever.

As always, we appreciate reader input on this and future *Production Line to Frontline* volumes, and the author would be pleased to receive comments, suggestions, information and photographs at PO Box 6490, Woodland Hills, California, USA, 91365.

Michael O'Leary

Los Angeles, March 1999

CHAPTER 1

THE PROTOTYPE

AS LT BENJAMIN KELSEY surveyed the crumpled wreckage of the Lockheed XP-38 interceptor, he probably reflected on the radical aircraft's future with the Army Air Corps, as well as his own career. The circumstance of a lieutenant wrecking a brand new fighter was not a happy one – even though Kelsey had held that lowly rank for nearly ten years! That situation was not because of any incompetence on Kelsey's part, but rather the opposite, since he was one of the best test pilots in the Air Corps. Kelsey's lack or promotion was due entirely to the slow pace with which the Air Corps of the 1930s progressed.

There were few aircraft and few positions to fly them, so promotions were more than agonizingly slow – they were almost non-existent, even if individual pilots were rated more than outstanding. That fact did not help Kelsey on 11 February 1939, for the new and glistening aircraft that would have pushed the Air Corps into the forefront of military aviation was nothing more than scrap.

During the 1930s, the Air Corps was stocked with a curious collection of 'combat' aircraft. Many were 'O-birds' – lightly-armed observation craft that performed little in the way of function besides providing a platform for pilots to fly. The pursuits of the day were little more than glorified sports aero-planes, built for a war that would never happen, while strategic bombing rested on the broad fabric wings of aircraft whose design would not have been out of place during World War 1.

The Air Corps was not completely deaf to the appeals by far-sighted officers for new, dynamic aircraft, which would inject needed life into the service and provide America with a realistic defense capability. However, the government, which was still struggling with the disastrous effects of the Great Depression, was almost completely reluctant to supply the Air Corps with money for anything as frivolous as new aircraft.

From 1935 to 1937, the growing menace of a Hitler-dominated Germany began to register on even the most isolationist of American politicians, and some money began to flow from the depleted government coffers to the military for limited research and development on advanced aircraft projects.

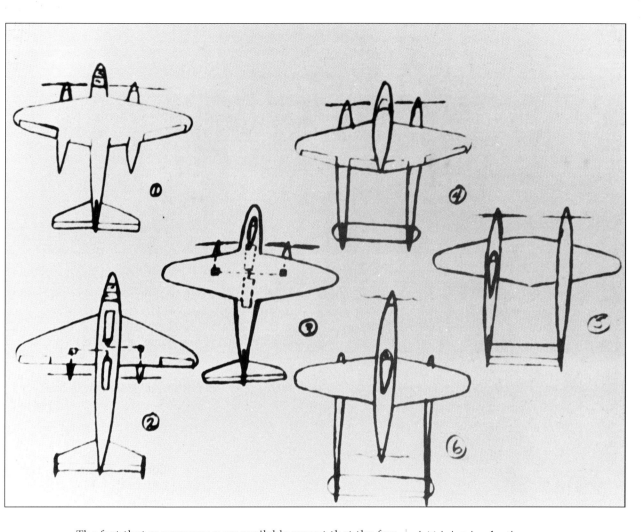

Initial sketches for the new aircraft that were considered by Hall Hibbard and 'Kelly' Johnson

The fact that money was now available meant that the few Air Corps officers who were concerned with aircraft development could now start voicing ideas as to the direction of fighter design. Observations in Europe had led to the idea that American aircraft development was much too conservative, and that funds should be allocated to companies which had designers who could creatively form new concepts and put them into production. One of the developmental projects envisioned was a twin-engined interceptor that would be capable of carrying a heavy armament to high altitudes, which would be achieved via new turbosupercharged engines that were also being developed.

The new design would have a long range, and be able to climb quickly in order to intercept high-flying bombers. Also, a tricycle landing gear was specified so that ground handling could be simplified. The requirement was given the title of 'Specification X-608' and circulated among interested aircraft manufacturers – which effectively meant virtually all aircraft builders, since the industry was in a depressed economic condition, and military contracts were subject to aggressive competition. The specification was spearheaded by none other than Lt Kelsey, an MIT graduate who, in 1934, had been

appointed officer-in-charge of the Fighter Projects Office at Wright Field – he was also the *only* officer in the office!

One of the companies that was deeply interested in the 1937 specification was Lockheed Aircraft Corporation. The company, located in rural Burbank, California, had gone through numerous ups and downs over the past decade as the poor worldwide economy decimated the aviation manufacturing community. However, Lockheed had developed a reputation for designing and building high-performance aircraft that offered advanced aerodynamics, and an ability to grab records and headlines. Pilots of the calibre of Amelia Earhart, Wiley Post and Howard Hughes had flown Lockheed aircraft such as the Vega and Lodestar to garner new speed and distance records. Nevertheless, profits were small and for several years the company operated 'in the red'. The Models 10, 12 and 14 airliners were gaining acceptance among the growing air transport system, but lucrative government contracts were needed to assure stability and growth.

An earlier Air Corps specification (which eventually resulted in the construction of a limited number of Bell FM Airacuda 'bomber destroyers') had led Kelsey into contact with Lockheed and chief designer Hall Hibbard, and his young assistant Clarence 'Kelly' Johnson. Kelsey was impressed with the aircraft the men created for the proposal (it was Johnson's first crack at a military design), but Bell won the contract by the narrowest of margins and built the Airacuda, which turned out to be supremely unsuccessful. 'Kelly' Johnson had been hired as a graduate from the University of Michigan in 1933, after

The XP-38 parked on the ramp at March Field, Riverside, California, during January 1939. Although the aircraft would retain its basic shape throughout its production life, thousands of minor and major changes would be made to the airframe. Sadly, this trend-setting prototype was extremely poorly photographed – whether by intent or just through a lack of time is not known

Hibbard had been impressed by a (critical) report that 'Kelly' had written on a Lockheed transport. Johnson would go on to have what could reasonably be described as one of the most impressive careers in American aviation, designing such diverse aircraft as the U-2, F-104 and the stunning SR-71. However, in 1936 Kelly was still 'proving his stuff', and looking forward to bringing some of his radical aeronautical concepts to fruition.

Lockheed had been considering a high-performance military aircraft prior to the specification being issued, and had come up with a working proposal for the new machine, which was designated the Model 22 (also identified in period documents as Project M-12-36). The design inception date was March 1936. At this point, Lockheed was a small company with 1200 employees and just 50 design staff.

Johnson looked at Specification X-608 with a critical eye and realised that the biggest handicap would come from the lack of a suitable powerplant. The Air Corps required the new aircraft to climb to 20,000 ft in six minutes and offer a top speed of at least 360 mph at altitude. Long range was also required, and all fuel had to be carried internally – this would later cause problems. Working with Hibbard, 'Kelly' immediately began making sketches of proposed aircraft.

The interesting common denominator of these early drawings was that all of the sketches had two engines. One engine would simply not provide the performance for the top speed or the rate of climb required by the military. 'Kelly' was always one to keep aircraft designs as sleek as possible, and he duly chose the V12 Allison V-1710, since it could develop at least 1000 hp

Since photos of the XP-38 are rare, the Air Corps had this rather fanciful composite 'flight' view made – complete with speed streamers – to show the XP-38 'on the wing'. As far as can be determined, neither Lockheed or the Air Corps actually photographed the prototype in the air

(with good growth potential), while at the same time offering a low frontal area due to better streamlining. It was also the only high horsepower American inline engine in series production.

Initial sketches showed a wide variety of possible configurations – combined pusher and puller engines, all pushers or all pullers with engines on the wing, or buried in the fuselage. Lockheed had been considering a high-performance military aircraft for the past year to be produced as a private venture in the hope of capturing a military contract, so useful contacts had already been made with influential Air Corps officers (including Kelsey). They were given 'previews' of the new design in order that the company could benefit from their criticism.

The attention of Hibbard and Johnson rapidly settled on the 'paper' aircraft that had elegant twin booms, with a fuselage pod mounted on the wing between the booms. Power was to come from twin Allison V-1710-C series engines that could produce a maximum of 1150 hp each, and high-altitude performance would be greatly enhanced by twin General Electric turbosuperchargers located in the booms and connected to the engines through a complex system of tubing. Tricycle landing

This close-up view of the installation of the XP-38's right hand Allison shows the design team's dedication toward streamlining, the V12 engine being cowled as closely as possible. Indeed, the handmade cowlings for the XP-38's would have looked more at home on a one-off racing 'special' than a prototype military aircraft. Of note is the extremely fine metal work on the handmade aircraft gear – the nose gear in the fuselage pod and the main gear in the spacious booms – was provided to help ground handling. Another novel feature was having all armament situated in the forward nose. The armament was not immediately finalised since a variety of cannon were under consideration, but by putting all armament in the nose, a concentrated stream of lead and high explosive could be accurately aimed at an enemy, with devastating results.

Another important milestone with the Model 22 design was that the structure was designed for a butt-jointed, flush surface, skin to give maximum streamlining. Also, the Model 22 would be the first production aircraft to have all its flight controls covered in aluminum rather that the traditional fabric. It is also interesting to note that the original Lockheed concept did not call for contra-rotating propellers. After Johnson had completed the majority of the design work for an elegant thin airfoil wing, this had to be abandoned when he found that there was just no way the Air Corps' fuel requirement could be contained within the wing – and the service refused to consider external tanks! This resulted in the Model 22 having a thicker wing which, in many ways, resulted in less performance. In his

Detail view of the strong, and relatively simple, engine mount holding one of the XP-38's Allison V-1710s in place. The large tube device immediately below the mount is the oil temperature regulator

final report (No 1152) on the new design, Johnson devoted six pages to 'Compressibility Effects', since he knew the new aircraft would be entering into untested territory.

Kelsey carefully went over the proposals tendered by Lockheed and other companies (including Bell). Impressed by the sheer power represented by the Model 22, he recommended, after Lockheed president Robert Gross hand-delivered the Model 22 drawings to Kelsey during February 1937, that the Air Corps issue a prototype contract to the Burbank firm. Bell's design also won a single-engine prototype contract, and their design would in turn become the XP-39.

After further consideration, the government issued Air Corps Contract Number 9974 to Lockheed on 23 June 1937 for the construction of one XP-38 that would carry the Air Corps serial 37-457. Cost of the aircraft was listed as $163,000. The company was pleased to receive the order, although they realised that the new XP-38 was radical, and one aircraft might not lead to production if the design did not perform correctly. Johnson, ever the optimist, predicted that the XP-38 would fly at 400 mph, some 40 mph faster than the speed the Air Corps calculated. The magic figure of 400 mph really appealed to the Air Corps, since a very high top speed would help impress Congress when it came to ordering more aircraft.

The in July 1938 the company commenced sub-assembly

A mock-up of the fuselage pod was utilised whilst the actual XP-38 was being built right alongside. Once the former had been completed, it was used to check the positioning of controls and instruments prior to finalising the layout of the prototype. Unlike most other fighters of the period, the Lightning had a large control yoke rather than the more traditional control column

construction of the XP-38 in a partitioned portion of one of their Burbank hangars, and workers had to overcome initial problems fitting and flush riveting the aluminum skin of the aircraft – this was a truly state-of-the-art machine, and a learning curve had to be achieved as the prototype was built.

As 'Kelly' moved up the company ladder, Jim Gerschler took over as project engineer. He quickly effected some detail changes, including the addition of Allison V-1710-C7 and C9 engines, which would have contra-rotating propellers that would virtually eliminate the torque effect. The right engine would turn in the opposite direction to the left engine, resulting in its propeller spinning in a clockwise direction to counter the torque forces of the left propeller. This meant that the pilot would not have to put up with the tremendous pulling force created by the torque of two engines turning in the same direction on take-off and landing. Gerschler also produced a series of design drawings featuring the installation of either a 23 mm Madsen cannon or .90-cal T1 cannon.

The Model 22 was classified as a secret project, so access to the area was limited, but most employees certainly knew what was going on – a far cry from the company's now famous 'Skunk Works', created by none other than 'Kelly' Johnson to develop very classified projects. However, the start of the XP-38 project could be considered as the birth of the 'Skunk Works', for the same crew that worked on this aircraft would also develop and build the XP-80 Shooting Star, which the company considers as the official 'Skunk Works'' starting point.

For a fighter, the XP-38 was certainly like nothing else that had flown in America. First of all, it was just plain *huge*. Weighting in at a bit over 15,000 lbs, and with a wingspan of 52 ft, the XP-38 looked more like a stylised bomber than a pursuit aircraft. Lockheed had come up with a beautifully sleek installation for the twin Allisons, and the cowlings were so snug that they would have been more at home on the front of a custom-built European racing machine. All the latest aeronautical technologies had been employed in building the airframe. The flush riveting was first-rate, the polished metal barely marred by any sort of bump or protrusion that could harm streamlining. Lockheed workers were especially proud of what they had built, and the finished XP-38 reflected their dedication.

Large Fowler flaps, employed by Lockheed with great success on their transport aircraft (business for which had picked up considerably – especially since the British were placing large orders for a modified transport that was to gain fame as the Hudson bomber), were added to both the XP-38's wing sections in order to improve low-speed handling characteristics, while the installation of the large Allisons gave the engineers some headaches, since a failure of one engine while the aircraft was at slow speed (whilst taking off or landing, for example) could result in a crash.

The long, slim, booms that took the place of a 'normal'

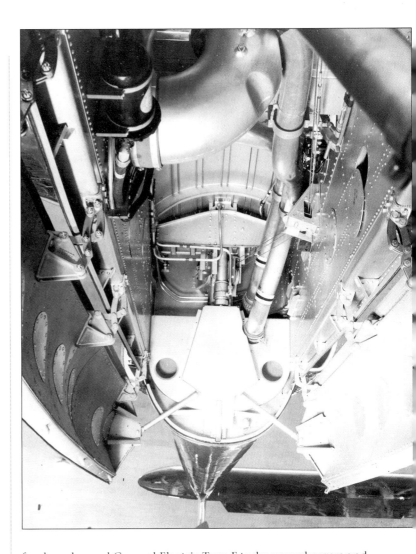

A detail shot of the 'plumbing' inside the left gear well of the XP-38. The interior of the aircraft was left unpainted

fuselage, housed General Electric Type F turbosuperchargers and the main landing, and supported the graceful twin tail unit that had now become almost a Lockheed trademark. The pod for the pilot was mounted on the very substantial wing centre section between the two engines. The nose landing gear was housed in the forward portion of the pod below the armament. The design crew liked the idea of centring the armament package (at this point, still undecided) for several reasons – ease of maintenance, a more concentrated cone of firepower could be achieved by a gathered battery of weapons compared to guns spread out over a wing, and the centre of gravity could be accurately maintained. As construction neared completion, the XP-38's armament was standardised on one 23 mm Madsen cannon and four Browning .50-cal M2 air-cooled machine guns with 200 rounds per gun. However, armament was never fitted to the prototype.

Unlike other fighters either in production or under development, the XP-38 was designed from the outset to have metal-covered control surfaces, rather than the more traditional fabric-covered units. Since the aircraft would be operating at high altitudes and at high speeds, the metal-covered surfaces would be more efficient when recovering from high-speed dives, as well as not being easily prone to damage. The controls were manually operated and dynamically balanced, but this would be changed later in the aircraft's life.

Lockheed, Allison, and General Electric worked closely together as the prototype was built to ensure that the operation of the engines at high altitude would be as efficient as possible. A complex network of tubing connected each engine to its individual turbosupercharger in the boom. The turbine wheel was located in a semi-flush housing atop each boom over the trailing edge of the wing, and as the aircraft gained altitude, the turbosupercharger would begin to function, taking exhaust gases from the engine to the turbine by means of the tubing system. The turbine would be spinning at tens of thousands of rpm, compressing the exhaust gases and passing them through an intercooler in the leading edge of the wing, and then channeling the compressed and cooled gas back down the throat of the engine to maintain manifold pressure at altitude. Such a complex system has to have problems, and the P-38 series would be bothered with developmental 'bugs' in the turbosupercharger system – but a more pressing problem was how to adequately cool the tightly-cowled Allisons.

The designers knew that the engines would have to be cowled as sleekly as possible so as to obtain maximum stream-lining, but the best location for the radiators and oil coolers posed a problem. Openings would have to be as large as possible so that cooling air could do its job but, at the same time, they would have to be as small as possible so that performance would not be degraded by the additional drag!

The XP-38 presented particular difficulties since it had two of everything. The radiators were located in the middle of the booms and were housed in large blisters that had their opening in the front and a control shutter at the rear, whilst the oil coolers were immediately behind the spinners. Once again, the cooling fluid (Prestone) had to be pumped from the radiator to the engine via tubing and a series of pumps, but this function did not provide completely adequate cooling, and overheating remained a problem throughout much of the P-38's career.

When basically completed, the XP-38 was trucked on 31 December 1938 from Burbank to March Field, in Riverside. The lengthy journey was accomplished with a great deal of secrecy, and the partially disassembled aircraft was wrapped in canvas to prevent prying eyes from getting a close view. As a major Air Corps base, March offered long runways and, in those days, was pretty much remote from major population centres. After the aircraft arrived, surviving its trip on mainly two-lane roads, several days were needed to assemble the machine, service it, and make sure all systems were up and operational. Lt Kelsey kept a close watch on the assembly of the XP-38, and made sure that he learned how the systems worked so that, hopefully, nothing would come as a surprise during the first flight.

The first step in finding out whether a new aircraft is ready for flight is a taxy test. During these tests, the aircraft is trundled down the runway at various speeds, and the pilot and crew hope that any possible flaw will be discovered at this time. Kelsey quickly found that the XP-38 had a number of disturbing problems, one of which almost resulted in the loss of the prototype even before it had flown. As the speed of the taxy tests increased, it became apparent that the XP-38 did not have sufficient braking power. Indeed, one high-speed taxy test resulted in the brakes becoming extremely hot and losing all function. Kelsey was sitting atop an out-of-control 15,000-lb monster that was rapidly 'eating up the remaining portion' of March's runway. The XP-38 shot off the end of the paved area and bounced through the grass and dirt, hit a ditch and stopped.

By the time Kelsey had unstrapped and clambered from the cockpit, Lockheed engineers had already arrived in speeding cars. The frightened team inspected their creation, running hands over the polished skin to feel for any deformation of structure. After a quick walk around, they were surprised and delighted to find no damage. Now, something had to be done about those brakes.

March Field was home to a variety of Air Corps bombers so, after the XP-38 was moved to one of the hangars, engineers did some scavenging through the Corps' spares bin and found items that could be put to use. Using a cylinder from a Northrop A-17 dive-bomber and an extra small tank to contain additional hydraulic fluid, the engineers attached the pump and tank inside the XP-38 so that when the brakes began to fail, the pilot could pump additional fluid into the brake reservoir, thus providing increased braking pressure and cooling.

This was an emergency 'lash-up', however, as both Kelsey and Lockheed realised that the brakes would be good for only one or two landings. The former decided that the best way of getting the XP-38 safely back on the ground would be to bring the big fighter in over the fence at the slowest possible speed – right on the edge of the stall – so that the aircraft could use the entire runway to stop with minimal braking. Both entering a new phase in high performance aerodynamics, Kelsey and the Air Corps soon learned that dragging an aircraft in over the runway threshold at a very low speed was both unwise and unsafe.

Work and maintenance was finally completed on 27 January 1939, and on a clear California morning, the XP-38 was pulled from the hangar and a series of final checks began. The aircraft looked truly beautiful in its polished and waxed natural aluminum finish, the only markings being the colourful pre-war Air Corps red, white and blue rudder stripes and the blue cockade, white star and red centre painted on the outer wing panels. Even the three-blade Curtiss propellers had been carefully polished. The attention to detail on the XP-38 was very evident, the handmade cowlings being wrapped tightly around

This Lockheed painting of the XP-38 was prepared for an advertising campaign that was quickly dropped after the well publicised crash of the prototype

the Allisons, while every item that protruded into the slipstream had been made as small as possible, and this included the air scoops and radiators.

Kelsey, dressed in the standard Air Corps garb of the period, boarded the prototype, went through a brief engine check to keep temperatures in the green (the engines had been run by mechanics before he boarded the aircraft) and began to taxy toward the runway using the rudders for directional control, and staying off the brakes as much as possible. Slowly, but positively, advancing the large throttles with his left hand while feeling the speed build up through the big control column and yoke, Kelsey made the decision to go after rolling about 200 ft. Speed quickly built up, and a tug on the yoke lifted the nose wheel free of the concrete and the XP-38 climbed smoothly away from the runway – the roar of its twin Allisons a muted rumble as the exhaust gases passed through the turbosuperchargers. However, it was not to be a smooth flight, and only Kelsey's skill would save the new fighter from destruction.

The crumpled remains of what the press called the 'Army's mystery plane' on a golf course adjacent to Mitchel Field, Long Island, New York, on 11 February 1939 after Lt Ben Kelsey's cross-country speed run. The beautifully crafted prototype was not considered worth rebuilding and was scrapped

Just after the main wheels lifted from the runway, a dreadful flutter set in, causing the instrument panel to disappear in a violent blur. Fighting to maintain control with the vibrating yoke that was trying to shake itself out of his hands, a quick glance out of the cockpit nearly caused Kelsey's heart to stop – the wing tips were shaking so violently that they were traveling three feet up and down!

Kelsey grabbed the flap handle and yanked the flaps up – the large Fowler flaps had been half down, a procedure for take-off that had been recommended by Lockheed engineers. As the flaps came up into the wing, the intense flutter stopped – only Kelsey was still shaking.

Reducing speed and keeping the nose raised, Kelsey flew the XP-38 near March Field for 34 minutes – making the gentlest of manoeuvres and trying to figure out what caused the fighter to nearly shake itself to pieces. During the intense flutter, the pilot had noticed a portion of flap shaking particularly violently. The fact that the flutter had disappeared when flaps were retracted led him to attempt a landing with the flaps in the full up position. Since the flaps had to stay up, Kelsey was forced to keep the fighter's nose at about an 18° up angle during the approach, and the fins of the twin rudders contracted the runway before the main wheels.

Once back on the ground and safely stopped, the XP-38 was minutely examined and the cause of the flutter was immediately discovered. Three of four soft aluminum control rods for the flaps had broken due to the intense flutter which, in turn, had come about from a lack of gap sealing and poor flap installation. This matter was quickly rectified by adding steel control rods, cutting away some parts of the wing skin and providing adequate gap sealing for the flaps. Damage to the fins was also repaired. Still, the flap arrangement was far from ideal, but the engineers modified the flaps sufficiently on later aircraft to get rid of the problem.

It was a matter of great urgency that the testing programme rapidly continue, so by 10 February the XP-38 had completed five additional flights, accruing nearly five hours of flying time. With the flutter gone, Kelsey found the XP-38 to be a dynamic aircraft which handled quite well considering its size. Further developmental problems occurred with the engines and turbo-superchargers, but this was to be expected, and both Lockheed and the Air Corps felt they had a winner on their hands.

Official Air Corps testing of new aircraft was carried out at historic Wright Field near Dayton, Ohio, so the XP-38 would have to be transported to that location. Lockheed reasoned that too much time would be involved by taking the prototype apart and shipping the aircraft by rail, so Kelsey decided the easier way to get to Dayton would be by air. To gain some positive publicity at the same time, the Air Corps decided that Kelsey should attempt to set a speed record between Los Angeles and Dayton. A fuel stop at Amarillo, Texas, was planned.

Fully fuelled, the XP-38 departed March Field on 11 February 1939, and Kelsey was going to rely on its cruise performance and not push the engines or the airframe in order to set a record. Quickly into the flight profile, the pilot realised that the XP-38 was really moving, and he arrived in Amarillo in just two hours and 48 minutes. Rapidly refuelling, Kelsey took just a further two hours and 45 minutes to reach Dayton. Chief of the Army Air Corps, Gen Henry 'Hap' Arnold, was on hand to greet the aviator and discuss the flight. Gen Arnold had been under pressure to get the Air Corps in the news with positive items. The European air forces were setting records constantly, and the Army needed a morale boost that would also be useful in obtaining contracts for new aircraft.

The cross-country speed record was, at that time, held by eccentric millionaire pilot Howard Hughes. Since a cross-country speed dash was not considered from the start of the XP-38 flight, the time spent on the ground at Amarillo meant that Hughes' overall record could not be beaten, but his total hours in the air record could be taken if the Air Corps acted quickly. After a brief discussion, Arnold said 'take it', and the aircraft was on its way to Mitchel Field, Long Island, New York, as soon as fuel and oil supplies were replenished. The wisdom of sending such a new, and basically untested, prototype on a further distance flight almost certainly contravenes today's strict aeronautical testing rules, but procedures were much more lax in 1939.

Averaging 360 mph, a tired Kelsey began his descent into Mitchel Field when the carburettors began, apparently, to pick up ice. 'Carb' ice comes about in certain weather conditions when, with the engines at reduced idle, ice begins to form in the throat of the carburettor and, if the ice builds up enough, the fuel supply to the engine can be choked off. Most aircraft are equipped with carburettor heaters (a system that supplies heat to the 'carbs' when the engines are at reduced power or in weather conditions likely to produce ice), but the XP-38 did not boast such a luxury. Kelsey did not know that the deadly ice had started to form in the 'carb' throats during descent. Kelsey

Examining a model of the XP-38 for the cameras, Ben Kelsey enjoys a few moments of relaxation after the accident. He soon got back on track, and continued promoting the P-38 to Air Corps officials

carefully brought the flaps down, reduced power even further and raised the nose in order to bring the XP-38 in as slow as possible, since the braking system was still less than adequate.

As he approached the runway threshold, the pilot saw that he was a bit low and he eased the throttles forward and was faced with the shocking realisation that there was almost no power (see sidebar opposite). The forward movement of the throttles produced little response from the engines, and the XP-38 was destroyed when it slammed into the ground short of the runway threshold. Kelsey escaped with minor scrapes.

Lockheed and the Air Corps were now faced with the problem of having an interesting concept but no hardware to back up the programme. The Air Corps reconsidered the aircraft and, on 27 April 1939 instigated a contract with Lockheed for 13 service test YP-38 aircraft. Hap Arnold had been one of the supporters of the programme, and he campaigned with the government for the new aircraft. The fact that the contract was issued so quickly really was due to the persuasive nature of Arnold's argument. The XP-38 had never really produced any performance or combat data that the Air Corps could study and consider, and they were basically taking the word of one man, relying on his uncanny judgment that Lockheed could produce what the Air Corps needed.

PILOT'S STATEMENT

*As per standard procedure, the Air Corps made
Lt Ben Kelsey recall his accident with the XP-38, and
the document is printed below;*

Departed from Wright Field at 3:25 pm; accident occurred while attempting landing at Mitchel Field at 4:50 pm. Arriving over New York at 14,000 ft, the engines were throttled to lower power, about 15 inches manifold pressure. The engines were running at this partial power for about three minutes and then throttled down and the plane slowed to get the gear down. After lowering the gear, partial power about 20 inches manifold pressure and about 2000 rpm was used in the turn for approach. The engines were throttled completely and the plane slowed to about 120 mph to lower the flaps. After the flaps were down, the throttles were opened. The left engine started up partially, but the right continued to idle. The fuel capacity was checked, fuel pressure was steady at four pounds on both engines. Mixture controls were rich; the left engine was running at about 15 inches and 1900 rpm. The prop pitch was checked to be sure it was in low pitch.

When it became obvious that with gear and flaps both down the plane would not glide into Mitchel Field, the flaps and gear handle were put in the UP position in the hope that with less drag it might coast in. When the speed got down under 120, further efforts to get one engine to go were abandoned, since with the low speed and high drag, the plane obviously could not be held if one engine came on full. The glide was slowed to about 100. It appeared that it might glide to a golf course across the road from Mitchel Field. As the trees were approached, the speed was kept at 90 to 95 and after passing through the tops of the trees, it was pulled up sharply just before hitting. It landed in a normal altitude in the bottom of a gully and slid up the bank. There was an impression that the main gear hit while partially extended. All items on the check list were checked on approach. The flaps were intentionally lowered so as to undershoot a little, figuring on pulling in with the engines so as to make the shortest possible landing due to the long ground run of the plane. The engines have to be completely throttled to get the flaps down without causing vibration through the middle range.

Of the possible causes, the most likely seems to be the possibility of icing in the carburettors due to excessive intercooling at high speed and partial power. As far as could be ascertained in the time available, there was no apparent reason either in the operation of the controls or in the instrument indications of any mechanical failure or engine failure as such. The fact that both engines were partially out indicates that some general condition must have affected both. There is no control for carburettor heat since these engines have never given indication of icing, and with turbo installations there is normally sufficient heat or compression. However, in this case, the high-speed, lower power condition may have cooled the air below normal conditions.

Benjamin S Kelsey
1st Lieutenant, Air Corp

CHAPTER 2

TESTING AND COMPRESSIBILITY

WITH THE PROTOTYPE IN RUINS, Hap Arnold and other influ-ential Air Corps officer lobbied long and hard for Lockheed's new fighter, and this resulted in a contract being issued on 27 April 1939 for 13 YP-38s. The 'Y' in the designation denoted that the new aircraft would be used for service test and evalua-tion in preparation for the type's entry into operational service. The fact that the contract was issued so quickly was due to the persuasiveness of Arnold's argument. The XP-38 had crashed essentially unproven, and the Air Corps was basically taking the decision based on the word of just a few men, who were con-vinced that Lockheed could produce what was needed.

Contract 12523 spelled out the terms for the production of the YPs, but the YP was to be vastly different from the XP, and problems were to develop accordingly. Lockheed gave the YP-38 the new company designation Model 122, and the engineering team went to work refining and developing the basic design, which would need extended development to make it into a combat-ready fighter.

Amongst the many changes were the installation of the latest variants of the Allison V-1710 engine, namely the F series -27 (F2R) and -29 (F2L), which had both propellers turning out-board in an effort to reduce airflow turbulence over the tail sur-faces. If both engines were operating correctly, then the effect of torque would be effectively counteracted. British contracts for Hudson had brought new prosperity to Lockheed, and the com-pany management had enough sense to see that aviation's dark age was at an end, and massive orders for military aircraft were in the very near future.

Oddly, this optimism did not extend to the P-38, and com-pany officials felt that the Air Corps would not order more than 80 aircraft, and that this would lead to later problems in adapt-ing the design for mass production. The company made plans to rapidly expand, and nearby buildings (including a distillery) were purchased while construction was started on new facilities. An intensive drive was also undertaken to hire and train new workers (up to 500 workers a day were being hired during 1941).

The distillery was converted to handle the production of P-38 sub-assemblies and the building of the YPs, but the expan-

sion proved to be so rapid that work began to flag on the YPs, and even though initial drawings had been approved and released by mid-1939, actual fabrication work did not begin until early 1940. As the plant expanded in a rather disjointed manner, delivery clerks had to resort to the use of roller skates to deliver blue prints and documents between the diverse hodgepodge of buildings!

Lockheed President Robert Gross, with an eye on the future, began acquiring land around the airport, and he even purchased the field outright from United Airlines. The latter acquisition also included several hundred acres of land, and resulted in the airfield changing names from Union Air Terminal to Lockheed Air Terminal. As more orders poured in from the British for additional Hudsons and follow-on Venturas, Gross and his staff realised that the distillery would not be adequate for fighter production, and other plans were made.

Although XP-38 construction had proceeded at very fast speed, the YPs were dragging their feet as change after change had to be done to the technical drawings, as well as to partially completed airframes. During this critical period in history, time was something that was just not available in abundance.

France had fallen to the German *Blitzkrieg* by the end of

A magnificent landscape view of Marshall Headle taxying in a YP-38 past rows of camouflaged Hudsons (which look quite dowdy in comparison to the YP's gleaming elegance) slated for the Royal Air Force. At the Air Corps' insistence, external mass balances were added to the elevator, even though 'Kelly' Johnson had installed such devices internally

June 1940, leaving Britain alone, facing a hostile Europe across a small channel of water, and licking its wounds from the pounding that the British Expeditionary Force had taken at Dunkirk. Aircraft were being built by the hundreds and pilots trained as fast as possible, but the Royal Air Force appeared to be ill-prepared to meet the *Luftwaffe* in aerial combat.

Air Corps officials watched the unfolding events in Europe with grave concern, and attempted to spur Lockheed and the production of the new fighter. However, the first YP-38 did not fly until 17 September 1940 when test pilot Marshall Headle took the fighter up from Burbank for a short proving flight.

Although the YP looked a great deal like the XP, it was in many ways a new aircraft, and the Air Corps knew that testing would have to be intensive to prove the design ready for military service. Also, the Air Corps was concerned about overall weight, and specified that the YPs weigh 1500 lbs less than the XP, imposing further design problems since weight tends to increase as aircraft become closer to being produced to military standards. However, the flow of YPs from the factory was not especially fast, and this put the programme in some jeopardy. The 13th YP was not delivered until May 1942, but test pilots had begun building up flying hours on the type, and new problems were soon to develop.

The weight of the YP-38 came in at 11,171 lbs empty and 13,500 lbs with a normal load, so the design team had been able to knock the weight down a bit, but not as much as the customer desired. Weight was not to be the main problem once the flight test programme for the YPs had started, however.

A new and frightening aerodynamic force called compressibility came into focus. Defined, compressibility means that as

The first YP-38 is rolled out of the modest Building 214 for the benefit of the press corps. As can be seen, the aircraft was highly polished and featured two tubes protruding from the nose – these where the positions for two .50 cal machine guns (never installed), while the nose also housed three other gun ports. The armament of the aircraft underwent numerous studies, and at this point it was decided to fit the aircraft with two .50 cal weapons with 200 rounds per gun (rpg), two .30s with 500 rpg and one Browning M9 37 mm cannon with 15 rounds – however, all that would change. Note that cuffs for the propellers had yet to be fitted

an aircraft travels faster through the atmosphere, air molecules begin to compress around certain points of the airframe. If the compression occurs around vital control surfaces, then the flying quality of the aircraft can be drastically affected, and this is what happened to the YPs.

Lockheed test pilots such as Jimmy Mattern (holder of some impressive long-distance flight records set in the 1930s in a Lockheed Vega) had been carrying out brief check flights in the YPs prior to them being turned over to the Army for extensive evaluation. One of the Air Corps' favourite manoeuvres of the period was popularly called the 'power dive', and this would involve a pilot taking the aircraft up to altitude and then pushing the nose over and diving as fast as possible to see how it would handle, and then recover. It was not uncommon for prototype aircraft *not* to recover, or to break up from the great pressures exerted in pulling up from a power dive, so test pilots were really earning their salaries on these flights.

During one such flight, Maj Signa Gilkie (an experienced Air Corps test pilot) had taken a YP up to 35,000 ft for a planned dive at over 400 mph. At this point, the aircraft had just been

Marshall Headle displays the first YP to advantage for the cameras. The YP was extensively photographed so as to make up for the almost complete lack of good photography of the XP. This view shows the distinctive P-38 shape – something that would not change over its production life, even though thousands of detail changes and modifications would take place. Note that the external mass balances had not been fitted to the elevator

Marshall Headle administers oxygen to Milo Burcham before a high-altitude test flight. Note the early high-altitude flight suit and homemade crash helmet (covered with stars!), which were very unusual for the period. Tragically, Headle would soon receive serious injuries in Lockheed's pressure chamber which ended his flying career, and resulted in his early death before the conclusion of the war. Headle had been a consummate test pilot, carefully proving the worth of many of Lockheed's early designs before progressing to the P-38, and a whole new field of aerodynamics

cleared for dive tests. However, the flight did not go as planned, and as the aircraft accelerated in the dive, Maj Gilkie suddenly found the yoke wildly bucking as he attempted to hold on to the controls. As the YP passed through 400 mph, it seemed to the pilot that its elevator had gone into extreme flutter. It also appeared that the nose was starting to tuck under, giving Gilkie the sense that the fighter was about to go over on its back.

All of these near-uncontrollable flight characteristics were directly caused by the compression of airflow over the aircraft's centre section, which in turn resulted in the creation of very turbulent airflow that was going through a venturi effect and producing the extreme tail buffeting. Fortunately, Maj Gilkie retarded the throttles and used the elevator trim tab to fight the aircraft out of what was a near-fatal situation. Compressibility had been encountered, but hardly anyone knew what to do about this disturbing effect.

Lockheed test pilots duplicated the dive and found the same problems. External mass balances were installed on the elevator, which was also reskinned with a thicker aluminum gauge. However, the problems continued, and 'Kelly' Johnson would report, 'The results of tests on all of the balance weights were that absolutely no change in indicated airspeed at which the vibration developed could be noted. The violence of the

vibration was unchanged, and the diving tendency was naturally the same for all conditions'. Wright Field instructed Lockheed that the fixing of the compressibility problem and tail buffet had to receive their immediate attention, but the company knew that a quick solution would be possible.

By September 1941, with the prospect of P-38 production being terminated if a solution could not be found, YP-38 c/n 2202 USAAC 39-689 (the first of its type completed) was assigned to the flight test department in order to solve the compressibility problem. Milo Burcham, Jimmy Mattern and Ralph Virden skillfully went about their flying, but were concerned when engineers wanted them to take the YP past 300 mph at 30,000 ft which, when factoring in the altitude, was beyond the YP's limiting Mach number of M 0.68. By this time the YP had received numerous modifications, including large elevator servo tabs that came into operation in order to help the pilot recover from the dive once forces on the yoke exceeded 30 pounds.

Despite the tabs, Burcham and Mattern remained reluctant to carry out the high altitude/high speed tests, but Virden agreed to give them a go. At this time he was a very experienced aviator, having amassed over 15,000 hours of flying time piloting airliners and working for the US Postal Service.

On 5 November 1941, over 25,000 Lockheed workers

Line-up of variously completed YP-38s receive service on the Lockheed ramp. The aircraft featured distinctively pointed spinners in comparison with their more blunted counterparts fitted to production models. With the installation of Allison's F-model engine, the powerplant package was re-engineered to make mass-production easier, and this included expanding the cowling and raising the thrust line

gathered at lunch time to hear a speech from Maj Gen Hap Arnold, who was now the new head of the Air Corps. This was at a time when production P-38s were now coming off the line, but the compressibility problem had yet to be resolved. Arnold was extremely upbeat, however, congratulating the workers on the great job that they were doing. While this was going on, P-38s, Hudsons and Venturas flew overhead, and when the speech was over, employees went back to work, and Virden completed the preflighting of the dive-test YP.

Ground checks over, the test pilot started the Allisons, taxied and took off. He was soon climbing out to the west from the Lockheed Air Terminal for his series of test dives, and these were apparently completed successfully, for the YP was back over the Burbank area 15 minutes later. Numerous eye-witnesses on the ground recorded what happened over the next few minutes. The YP was seen in a dive, making an unearthly shriek, followed by its fluttering tail assembly, which had broken off in flight. Even 'Kelly' Johnson heard the YP's fatal dive from his office, recalling later that the sound probably came from the propellers hitting the air at angles outside the 'realm of a normal flight path'.

Milo Burcham in a YP over Pasadena, California. Even though the cowlings had been expanded for the aircraft, they were still of an elegant shape . . . and an extremely tight fit. Note Milo holding the large control wheel, and the mass balances fitted to the elevator

The fighter crashed into a house at 1147 Elm Street in neighbouring Glendale, literally blowing the dwelling in half, and killing the pilot on impact. Fire and police officials reacted quickly, and once at the burning house, they expected to find fatalities only. However, owner Jack Jensen was discovered asleep in his bed – completely unaware that the Air Corps' latest fighter had destroyed his house!

Why had the YP crashed? Some said Virden was 'grand-standing' for the employees, but the noon-time rally was over and work had resumed. Also, the experienced Virden knew that a lower level dive would be fraught with danger. 'Kelly' Johnson finally came up with the most logical answer when, after examining the wreckage and data, he concluded that linkages to the larger elevator tabs failed, causing them to go into extreme deflection, which probably resulted in a sudden, and catastrophic, force travelling through the tail booms. This in turn caused an immediate structural failure of the units.

As production built up, the problems – and the testing – continued. A YP was flown to the wind tunnel at NACA's Langley Field facility, where it was subjected to numerous tests and modifications – including a lengthening of the fuselage pod in the hope of smoothing out the airflow (it didn't work). Johnson also continued working on the problem and, using his own data and that gathered from NACA at Langley, issued a report (*Study of Diving Characteristics of the P-38*) in early 1942 which attempted to cure the problem by calculating air speeds for the following steps:

1) The maximum speed that it is possible to attain in a vertical dive from the service ceiling, using military power.

Two record-breaking Lockheeds – an all-wood Vega of the late 1920s shares ramp space with a YP-38. This photo illustrates how far aerodynamics had progressed in just over a decade. However, for its time the Vega was a model of aerodynamic efficiency

2) The airspeed at which buffeting will start at an acceleration of 1G.

3) The airspeed at which the dive tendency is maximised.

4) The indicated airspeed at each altitude that is possible to attain in level flight.

5) From the preceding, the margin of speed available for manoeuvring without encountering either buffet or dive characteristics.

Johnson found that the P-38's drag factor rapidly increased as the airframe hit Mach 0.65. A shock wave formed around the wing's centre section, which in turn led to the tail buffeting. Lockheed was worried that modifications to the basic design would result in massive production delays, and once again place the future of the aircraft in doubt. Fortunately for all concerned, it would be a fairly minor modification that would effectively cure this shock wave problem – a small fillet was added at the juncture of the wing leading edge and the canopy. This unit had to be carefully installed to ensure a tight fit, but it also virtually eliminated the tail buffet.

As more P-38s poured from the factory, newer aircraft were allocated to the test role, and the classy YPs were relegated to training aids, before being scrapped before the end of the war. However, few that saw those gleaming thoroughbreds 'in the flesh' will ever forget the design that was propelling Lockheed into the future of advanced aerodynamics.

ABOVE YP-38 number two in the full-size wind tunnel at NACA's Langley Field facility in Virginia on 24 December 1941. At this point, the fuselage pod had been extended beyond the wing's trailing edge, but this did not help solve the tail buffeting or compressibility problems

LEFT The destroyed remains of Ralph Virden's YP-38 surround the house into which it crashed after the tail assembly came off the aircraft

CHAPTER 3 BRITAIN'S UNWANTED BUNDLE

THE NEW TWIN-ENGINED fighter from Burbank did not escape notice in Europe, and French and British Purchasing Commissions soon arrived at Burbank to be briefed on the P-38, and to visit the new production facility and view the technical staff at work. Both commissions liked what they saw, and orders – huge for the time – were placed. The French wanted 417 examples (to be designated Model 322-F) while the British opted for 250 Model 322-Bs during May 1940 (this was, of course, well before the first YP flew).

At this point, the French and British also had on order variants of the Curtiss Hawk 81 (fitted with the Allison V-1710C1-5) and, apparently for the sake of commonality, they wanted the new Lockheed fighter to be powered by the same engines *without* turbosupercharging. There was some logic to this specification, since General Electric was having huge problems delivering the units and, at that time, it appeared that much of the European air war would be fought at heights below 20,000 ft. They also asked for the engines to be geared so as to rotate the propellers in the same direction.

The deal was struck at the time of the 'Phoney War', which saw the Germans, having seized Poland in a matter of weeks, settling in 'for the winter' of 1939-40 to eye the Allied forces massed across the French border.

As part of the deal offered to Lockheed by the French and British purchasing commissions, the P-38s had to be delivered within one year, and both parties were willing to pay nearly $100,000,000 for the aircraft and spares. This was a stunning amount of money, and Lockheed agreed to the contract, despite company engineers surely being aware of the aircraft's sluggish performce at height without turbosuperchargers, and the unrealistic delivery schedule.

At this point, American aircraft usually received just numerical designations, and were rarely named. However, the British have always liked to name their aircraft, and these have ran the gamut from the ridiculous – the Tomtit – to the sublime – the Fury. For their Model 322-B, the British chose the appellation 'Lightning', and it was a name that would burn its way into aviation history.

ABOVE Revealing undersurface view of Lightning Mk I AE979, showing the slim engine nacelles and fuselage pod to advantage. One problem that remained with the Lightning throughout its production life was that the large nose gear door could 'creep' down as much as four inches during high-speed flight. Note the landing lights inboard of each RAF roundel

LEFT Some Lightnings scheduled for delivery to the RAF were retained by Lockheed after the cancellation of orders. This aircraft (the first Mk II built, serialled AF221) was refinished in standard AAF Olive Drab and Neutral Grey camouflage, and it is seen being tested as a mount for the aerial dispersal of chemicals

TOP Still painted in its well-worn RAF camouflage, and with a ground power unit plugged in, a Lightning Mk I (now redesignated an RP-322) has its engines run up prior to a test flight to evaluate new drop tanks (fitted on pylon stubs under the centre section). Several of the ex-RAF aircraft were retained at Burbank for various tests. Note that the fighter's armament has been removed and that the factory construction number on the nose has been crudely censored on the photograph. The polished panel on the inboard right cowling also appears to have been painted over – this part of the cowling was often left bare so that the pilot could visually check to see if the landing gear was down

ABOVE Again retaining its RAF camouflage, but with the addition of USAAF markings, Lightning Mk II AF221 (c/n 3244) was photographed at Burbank after it had been redesignated a P-38F-13-LO (USAAF s/n 43-2035). It was used for testing the Lightning's torpedo-carrying ability, and two concrete-filled dummies are seen attached to underwing pylons

Soon after the French order had been signed, Germany launched its *Blitzkreig* with such devastating effect that by the end of June 1940, France had totally capitulated. Accordingly, the French Model 322-Fs were added to the British order.

The first RAF Lightning Mk I did not fly until August 1941, and by this time the pivotal Battle of Britain had been won almost a year earlier, and aerial warfare was entering a new phase of high-altitude combat. British pilots stationed in America went to Burbank to fly the new fighter, and they were unanimous in their dislike of the British variant. Performance was considerably below specification, and above 12,000 ft the Lightning Mk I was deemed to be virtually useless as a fighter.

So rapid was the British condemnation of the Model 322 that only one example (RAF serial AF106) was ever shipped to Britain, where it was tested again with negative results. The fighter was reported to have good handling characteristics, but the restrictions on performance caused by the lack of a turbo-supercharger made the fighter of little use for aerial combat over Europe. The British were quick to cancel their large orders, but the Air Corps was equally quick to pick them up. A Lightning Mk II had also been planned, but only one example was finished in RAF markings before that order was also dropped.

Ironically, the Lightning Mk II had the more powerful Allisons, turbosuperchargers and other upgraded equipment, and these aircraft were also taken over by the Air Corps. The order comprised 524 machines, which were redesignated P-38Fs (150 Mk IIs), P-38Gs (374 Mk IIs) and P-322s (140 Mk Is). Most of the P-322s – a very unusual designation for an Air Corps aircraft – were sent through a re-engineering depot to receive more powerful Allison F-series engines, before being scattered around the country at various training bases. Others were retained at Lockheed for further test purposes.

Few student pilots remember the P-322 with any fondness since (even with the new engines) it was still underpowered, and boasted vicious engine cut-out characteristics. Quite a few P-322s were operated by the newly-redesignated USAAF in their RAF camouflage and serials.

Sprayed in a very worn Olive Drab and Neutral Grey camouflage finish, Lightning Mk I AF101 (redesignated RP-322) has its engines run at the massive USAAF depot at Newark, New Jersey, on 16 April 1946 – probably prior to being flown to a storage depot for scrapping. The 'R' in the RP-322 designation denoted that the aircraft was a restricted fighter (pursuit) trainer

CHAPTER 4 | INTO PRODUCTION

AS TESTING OF THE YP-38s continued, the first of 66 P-38s began to take form – this number being close to Robert Gross's original prediction that no more than 80 of the twin-engined fighters would be ordered by the Air Corps. The new contract had been issued on 20 September 1939 – even before the YP-38's first flight, and these new aircraft would be a mixture of P-38s, XP-38A and P-38Ds. Needless to say, everything was hectic at Lockheed as the company attempted to expand so as to fill the Air Corps' new orders, as well as the massive contracts recently signed with the British. Initially chaos reigned, but in the middle of all this tumult, order began to gain control and aircraft started regularly appearing from organised production lines.

One thing that was immediately noticeable about the new P-38s was their very purposeful look – gone was the glowing silver of polished aluminum, and in its place was the harsh reality of Dark Olive Drab (Shade 41) and Neutral Grey (Shade 43) camouflage applied according to Technical Order No 07-1-1. One paragraph of the new directive stated;

'Due to the highly pigmented content and dull finish of camouflage materials, camouflaged airplanes will not present as pleasing an appearance as the highly polished Alclad or glossy painted airplanes of the past. No attempt should be made to secure a polish or high gloss, as this will tend to defeat the purpose of the camouflage.'

The division between the two standard camouflage colours followed a wavy line from just under the nose cone to a point below the wing, where it moved up to meet the wing root. On the booms, the Olive Drab did not extend under the wings or tail, although it was brought down the trailing edge of the rudder almost to the join with the fin. Due to its nature, the camouflage rapidly weathered, and the tech order went on to state;

'Camouflage materials may have neither the adhesive nor the colorfast quality of specification paint materials used heretofore. It is anticipated that there will be minor chipping of the camouflage materials at the leading edges of the airfoils, particularly if the airplane is flown through heavy rains. This chipping may be somewhat unsightly, but as long as the material

ABOVE P-38F centre sections fill one of the assembly hangars. One of the more complex components of the Lightning, the cente section would, when completed, house the fuselage pod, engines, and main landing gear

LEFT Curtiss Electric propellers are readied for installation to Allison engines. Due to a lack of interior space, this work was being done on the Burbank ramp. The inability of Curtiss to deliver adequate numbers of propellers caused completed P-38Es to be flown to assigned bases, where the propellers were removed, placed in a C-47 and flown back to Burbank so the next group of P-38Es could be flown out! This was not an ideal situation, and was typical of the problems Lockheed was having with suppliers

ABOVE Workers swarm over a P-38D centre section, the massive construction of which is noteworthy. In the background, an RAF Hudson is being assembled

affords a reasonable coverage of the surface, the finish should not be touched up, as the chipping effect is not objectionable from a camouflage standpoint, and the additional weight derived through the continued touching-up process might become objectionable.'

Although the new fighters looked ready for combat, they were far removed from their assigned task.

The first P-38s were almost identical to the YPs except for some minor changes, while armament had been initially standardised on one 37 mm cannon and four .50 cal machine guns. Reports of combat in the skies over Europe were arriving on a daily basis (Air Corps test pilot Ben Kelsey had been shipped to Britain and France and saw first-hand what was going on, sending back a stream of messages to his superiors and Lockheed). It became obvious that the P-38s would need items such as armour plating and self-sealing fuel tanks.

The Air Corps issued a directive that P-38s on the production line would receive this equipment, and that they would be designated P-38Ds (36 were built as such). The 'D' suffix was used by the Air Corps to define fighter aircraft that had been brought up to the latest European combat standard. In addition to armour, self-sealing tanks and armoured glass for the windscreen, these aircraft had the less dangerous low pressure oxygen system installed, along with a retractable landing light. In an

ABOVE P-38Ds were completed in the California sunshine because all interior space was occupied, and new buildings were then still under construction. Although this view gives the overall appearance of chaos, order is apparent as items are methodically added to the airframes as they near the camera. In the background, RAF Hudsons are also being assembled. Although the latter aircraft have not been camouflage, national markings have been painted onto the airframes

LEFT As the war progressed, more and more women joined aviation production lines. This worker is running down a check list to make sure essential items have been installed as the P-38E moves closer to the flightline. Note the canvas nose wheel cover – each aircraft was issued with canvas wheel, engine and canopy covers

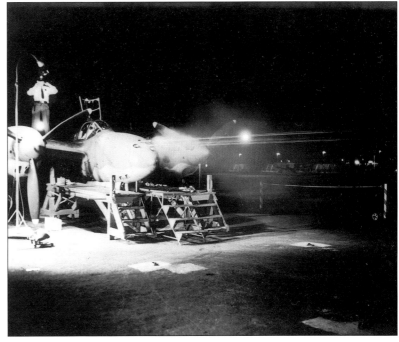

ABOVE P-38s in early stages of assembly, with noses and tail sections being completed. The Lightning production line would eventually become three-aircraft wide

RIGHT Work at Lockheed continued around the clock, and this P-38F is having its weapons tested in the dead of night. Note the security guard standing on the wing covering his ears

effort to keep the revised fighter's weight down, the maximum fuel capacity of these aircraft was reduced to 300 US gallons from 410 US gallons. Some of the P-38s and P-38Ds were set aside for research and development use, and some of the modifications carried out to these aircraft were very strange. For example, P-38 s/n 40-744 (the first built) had a cockpit installed in the left boom (the turbosuperchargers were removed from this aircraft) to test the effects of an asymmetrical layout on the pilot, whose sense of balance could have been disturbed by the placing of his position away from the aircraft's centreline.

Another aircraft was pulled aside for modifications, designated XP-38A and fitted with a pressurised cockpit. To help off-set the additional weight, production aircraft would have had the 37 mm cannon replaced by a 20 mm unit. Carl Haddon was the project engineer, and data from this experiment was applied to the XP-49. Joe Towle flew the aircraft from May through to December 1942, when it was handed over the the USAAF.

The Air Corps was not pleased with the tardy delivery rate for the new fighter, but this was not all Lockheed's fault, since they were experiencing delays with turbosuperchargers (General Electric), engines (Allison) and propellers (Curtiss). The construction of other sub-assemblies such as landing gear was also behind schedule, while the rapid expansion of buildings and the workforce had also caused problems. With P-38Ds

LEFT A female production line inspector uses her 'tools of the trade' (a mirror attached to the end of a 'wand' and a torch) to checks the installation of the armoured glass in a P-38F windscreen. Note that the glass is covered with a protective film

OPPOSITE TOP Spitfire Mk VA W3119 meets the Lightning. The former fighter was shipped to the USA in July 1941 (just months after being built), and was to subsequently spend its time touring various American aircraft plants to compare design philosophies, as well as undergoing flight testing at Wright Field and Langley. As can be seen, the Lightning dominated the RAF fighter in terms of physical size

RIGHT Lightning production at its best – three rows of P-38s head towards completion. Note the Allison QECs (Quick Engine Change units) ready for installation among the rows of parts bins

RIGHT Final assembly work on the rear portion of a P-38 canopy. This view gives some idea of the size of the component

BELOW A great deal of hand-fitting went into each cowl installation to insure a perfect match with the airframe assembly. This ensured that when panels were later removed for servicing in the frontline, re-attachment would take the minimum of effort

at last being added to the inventory, the Air Corps decided to send new fighters to the 1st Pursuit Group (PG) at Selfridge Field, in Michigan. Many of its pilots had flown the YP-38, and it was thought that experience gained on that type would help smooth the introduction of the P-38 into service.

The fact that P-38s were now in 'unit service' did not mean all that much, for when the 1st PG received their new mounts in the spring of 1941, the nose cannon had not yet been fitted and the aircraft was still some way from being combat ready. However, the 1st was prepared to test their new fighters in a realistic combat environment, and the twin-tailed P-38s went to Louisiana and the Carolinas for the extensive 'war games' which took place between September and November. Pilots were able to test their aircraft against other Air Corps machines such as the P-35, P-36 and P-40, and they found the P-38 to be generally superior in all categories, especially at high altitudes, where the other aircraft could not even hope to venture.

While the 1st PG was trying out its new mount, Lockheed was receiving further massive orders for the Lightning (the

British name was rapidly adopted by the company and, perhaps more importantly, by the press), and as 1941 drew to a close, more variants began to appear on the Burbank production line. On 30 August 1940, a follow-on contract for 410 aircraft had been issued by the Air Corps (to be delivered as P-38Es, P-38Fs, F-4s, F-4As, F-5s and F-5As), and Lockheed in turn placed massive subcontracts with suppliers which stretched their output capacity. Orders of this magnitude had simply never existed before.

The P-38E (Model 222-62-09) was the first major production version of the Lightning, and it was considered as an interim step towards the combat-ready P-38G. With the E-model, the 37 mm cannon was replaced by a license-built Hispano 20 mm weapon, and 150 rounds of ammunition. Once again many of the P-38Es were scattered to training units, but the Air Corps and Lockheed also retained some for modification and testing purposes. Those assigned to training units usually carried the 'R' prefix, indicating that the aircraft was for a non-combat role. Thus, the Air Corps operated RP-38s, RP-38Ds, and RP-322s as of 1942, when the designation change came into effect.

A typically busy day on the Lockheed flightline in 1942. B-17Fs, P-38Fs, Venturas and Lodestars undergo work prior to flight testing or delivery

ABOVE The 'Piggy-Back' P-38E was modified with several raised tails, and the second variant is seen here on 2 December 1942. This modification was for a projected floatplane version of the Lightning, the need for which evaporated after the first few Allied victories in mid to late 1942 in the Pacific

LEFT Having passed the wind-screen (see the photo on page 44), the inspector moves on to the starboard Allison installation on the P-38E. The mirror and torch were used to get into those 'hard to reach places'

Numerous RP-38Es were put to extremely strange uses. Some were converted into 'piggy-backs', as detailed elsewhere in this volume, whilst another was fitted with an upswept tail in the anticipation of the addition of floats, thus creating an aircraft that could be ferried long distances over water. The idea behind this was that P-38s could be flown to the Pacific theatre, have the floats removed on arrival in the frontline, and then resume their standard mission as land-based fighters. However, the US Navy's transportation system proved to more than adequate for shipping new fighters to combat bases, and this measure was dropped. Others were used to tow gliders, while 41-2048 was converted with dual controls (the only P-38 to achieve this status) and used to test various airfoil sections. Other P-38Es were modified to test out new drop tanks, while 41-1983 was used to trial features incorporated in the P-38J.

Along with the 377 Air Corps ordered machines, the P-38F series also incorporated 150 Lightning Mk IIs originally intended

P-38E s/n 41-2048 was used for a variety of tests, acquiring the nickname *Swordfish* at some point during its long career. This photo shows the aircraft being used to test airfoils, with a spray boom affixed aft of the left wing. The aircraft (with its extended fuselage pod) was first flown on 2 June 1943 by Tony LeVier, who found that it would dive faster than production P-38s. A splice of 30 inches was added to the front portion of the fuselage pod and 48 inches to the rear, which in turn created the space needed to house an engineer/observer

DROP TANKS

The original specification that led to the Lightning specifically ruled out the use of 'external' tanks. This caused a redesign of the wing, resulting in a thicker section so that all fuel could be held internally. As the aircraft went into service, it became obvious that external fuel was required for greater range, so Lockheed developed aluminium tanks, which sold for $678 apiece. However, by the middle of 1943 the company had developed droppable steel fuel tanks which almost doubled the aircraft's operational range, and cost the government less than $300 each. Weighing 90 lbs empty and 1000 lbs when filled with 165 gallons of avgas, they were designed so that two fully loaded tanks decreased the P-38's speed by about four per cent. A mammoth drawing press at the Weber Showcase and Fixture Co of Los Angeles performed the first operation in the construction of the ten-foot long, 27-inch diameter, tank. After the sheets of 24-gauge deep   drawing steel – measuring 48 x 144 inches, and weighing 41 lbs – were prepared, they were inserted one-by-one into the press. A ten-ton die, made of Mechanite iron, with a pressure of 500 tons, formed the halves.

Once the halves had been retrieved from the press, the outside flange – left by the operation – was hand-trimmed and the halves then inserted into a hydraulic press, which punched the locating holes as well as the holes which would receive the vents, filler plugs and drainage connections. This was accomplished in a single operation, saving approximately two hours in the manufacture of each tank.

The halves were then shipped to a branch plant of Lockheed for welding and finishing – all operations were handled through a conveyor system, which enabled the output of a tank every $4^{1}/2$ minutes, 24 hours a day!

This conveyor system was of the overhead type from which cradles were suspended, each cradle holding one tank, and the complete conveyor system holding 36 cradles. Welding and assembly equipment were located at various stations along the conveyor line in the sequence in which the operations were performed. The assembly conveyor was 475 ft long, ending on a freight platform, where the tanks were packed in a crate for shipping.

The first operation at Lockheed was the torch welding of the sump plug flange to the left hand skin, or shell. Next, the filler well adapter assembly was seamwelded to the same skin. The special series welder, designed by Lockheed, was similar to conventional series seamwelders such as those used in welding steel discs to shell forgings. However, it was somewhat unusual since the weld was made on a double contoured surface and had a rise of $3/4$ inch in 90° of rotation.

The machine was equipped with two air cylinders to which the shaft housing, welding shafts and welding wheels were connected. The two cylinders and welding units were electrically insulated from each other and bolted to a casting which rotated on a hollow shaft, mounted vertically. The inside diameter of this shaft was such that the water-cooled welding cables, which connected the two sides of the transformer secondary to the cast copper shaft housing, could be brought down through the shaft. The circular copper alloy short circuiting bar (the upper face of which was contoured to fit the inside of the tank) was mounted horizontally below the two welding wheels.

When the two wheels contacted the tank skin, the welding circuit was closed by the short circuiting bar. Since the welding current flowed through the sheets at two points, two welds were made simultaneously, and the 360° of welding was completed in approximately 185° actual rotation of the upper heads.

After this operation, bulkheads were then welded to both the left and right hand skins, seven to each shell. This was done in two semi-automatic welding machines. The first welded three bulkheads in place, whilst the second did the remaining four.

The half-shell was placed in the machine, where it was supported at the bulkhead stations by copper alloy electrode bars, which were machined to fit exactly the outside contour of the pressed-steel tank section. Lockheed incorporated into their design unique roll-spot welding units, which rotated about the longitudinal axis of the tank and were fastened to the hinged cover of the fixture that held the tank sections.

Each of these units consisted of a welding wheel and shaft, shaft housing, guide casting, three-inch diameter by $3/4$-inch stroke air cylinder, a $1/12$ horsepower driving motor, reducing gear box and the necessary gear train to drive the welding wheel shaft. The sequence panel and welding transformer were outside the fabricating jig proper.

The roller spot welds were controlled by units consisting of a Westinghouse non-synchronous pulsation-weld timer panel with a Weld-o-trol Electronic Contactor. These timers were modified slightly to secure the desired sequence of operation.

Except in the two centre bulkheads, where the welds were spaced at $1/2$-inch intervals, the welds were spaced $3/4$ of an inch apart, centre to centre. Welding time was just one minute in each of the two machines, with another minute being devoted to the loading and unloading of the freshly-welded shells.

Now the shells were placed on a moving conveyor. Flanged gussets and other parts which would hold the tank to the aircraft's pylons were located and spot welded to stressed bulkheads by a series of gun welders on monorails that enabled the operator to follow the tank along the floor until the individual's welding job was completed.

The two halves of the pan were seam-welded to the halves of the tank with a portable seam welder designed and constructed by Lockheed. This welder was supported from a Chicago Pneumatic counter balancer of 175 lbs capacity. The welding was done while the half tank was on the moving conveyor. Since the linear travel of the wheels on the welder was approximately the same as that of the conveyor, the wheels were designed to rotate in the opposite direction to that of the conveyor. The result was that the welder actually moved less than 18 inches during the welding process.

The halves were tackwelded together by a gun welder, and the tank was taken off the line, placed in a special cradle and run through a National Seamwelder that completed the mating operation. This seamwelding was done at the rate of 60 inches a minute, or a total of four minutes per tank.

Excess material on the standing seam was trimmed off with an electric shear, and the tail plug flange was torchwelded in place. The tank was then placed back onto the conveyor, where air pressure pumped inside and an application of soapy water outside tested the finished tank for leaks which, if present, were immediately repaired on the spot.

The tank was now ready for the slushing table, which held two tanks, one on each side. In each tank were poured 30 gallons of special non-inflammable zinc chromate primer. The table was so rotated that the fluid flowed over every portion of the inside of the tank, after which the tank was loaded onto a drying dolly and dried with a hot air hose.

Then the tank was given its final pressure test, the permanent tail plug was screwed in place and the tank placed onto the second, or process, conveyor. This conveyed it in turn through a hot Turco bath cleansing solution, a cold water rinse, a drying oven and a paint booth, where two primer coats and the final camouflage paint were swiftly applied.

This same conveyor then carried the tank into the shipping building where a female worker installed decals showing the manufacturer's name-plate, tank capacity, etc., and where anti-sabotage seals were placed over all openings. A protective coating of Paralketone was applied by spray gun, and the tank was then considered to be ready for crating.

A newly fitted-out P-38G cockpit

for the RAF. Retaining the same armament as the P-38E, the F-models were powered by 1325 hp Allison V-1710-49-53 engines. These machines were produced in five different batches, and each had its own set of updates and modifications. The F-series included the first Lightnings to carry drop tanks (F-5-LO), two 155/165 US gallon tanks being carried on pylons located between the engines and fuselage pod. Two 1000-lb bombs could also be fitted to these pylons in place of the tanks.

Built with 1325 hp Allison V-1710-51/55 engines, 708 P-38Gs (Model 222-68-12) were ordered in six blocks. These were generally similar to the F-series, but with numerous detail refinements which included an updated radio package, a new oxygen system, strengthened pylons that could carry a 1600-lb bomb apiece and winterisation equipment – useful both in the Aleutians and the European Theatre. The P-38G-13-LO and P-38G-15-LO (a total of 374 aircraft, designated Model 322-68-19) came from the British order for Lightning Mk IIs.

CHAPTER 5 XP-49

IT IS A CURIOUS TRUISM in the world of military development that when a new weapon enters service, it is probably already obsolete. This fatalistic attitude does hold credence, for in the field of aeronautics, today's development time for a new combat aircraft takes so long that, by the time the aircraft is in service, well over a decade has usually elapsed since the original thought crossed someone's mind.

During the 1930s, this time table was not so lengthy, but the amount of time between the creation of an idea and turning that idea into physical hardware was already rapidly increasing. The quickening pace of aeronautical technology was causing the Air Corps to worry, and they realised that plans for new aircraft had to be made *before* the aircraft they would replace were in service.

One of the items the Air Corps had been worrying about was the high price of their new P-38. Even though the Lightning looked like it was going to be a winner as the various developmental problems were met, and solved, by the Lockheed design team, the Air Corps was still having to labour under the hardship of a budget – even though that budget was increasing as the constraints of isolationism were abandoned.

In order to guard its position, the Air Corps issued Circular Proposal 39-775 on 11 March 1939 in the hope of finding an even better aircraft at perhaps an even lower price. However, the Air Corps was really grasping at straws in its search for the new long-range, twin-engined, fighter because the winner was to be none other than Lockheed!

In order to meet the new proposal, Lockheed designed the Model 522. The new fighter, one of four proposals submitted by manufacturers, looked very similar to the Model 222 – Lockheed apparently decided to capitalise on a winner. Contract W535-AC-13476 was issued on 30 November 1939 but it took until 8 January 1940 to finally execute the document.

The Model 522 was decidedly different from the second runner-up in the contest, the Grumman XP-50. A fairly straightforward machine with promise of future development, the XP-50 was destroyed during a test flight when one of its turbo- -

superchargers exploded and test pilot Robert Hall had to parachute from the flaming prototype as the aircraft plummeted into Long Island Sound.

Oddly, work on the XP-49 slowed as the P-38 built momentum, and as the Air Corps and Lockheed realised that the XP-49 would be overpowered with the proposed installation of the Pratt & Whitney XH-2600 or the Wright R-2160. During March 1940 the decision was reached to equip the new aircraft with the equally new Continental XIV-1430-9/-11 liquid-cooled 12-cylinder inverted V engine. The powerplant was rated at 1540 hp for take-off, whilst the other engines produced 2300-2500 hp. The adoption of the Continental meant that top speed would drop from a project 475 mph to around 400mph – basically the same as the P-38.

Construction of the aircraft proceeded at a slow pace. The original proposal envisioned a pressurised cockpit with two 20 mm cannon and four .50 cal machine guns. To get the aircraft going, consideration was given to drop the pressurisation requirement, but this was later reinstated. Also, dummy armour plate was to be installed rather than the real thing so that development could be moved forward. By late 1940 Lockheed was at last able to put enough staff on the XP-49 to get it moving, and under the leadership of Carl Haddon, a mock-up was completed at Burbank and inspected by the Air Corps on 28 August 1941.

Lockheed had come up with its own drum for the 20 mm cannon that would hold 90 rounds compared to the standard 60 rounds, but the Air Corps decided to go with the standard unit. Construction of the prototype moved ahead, but it soon became apparent that the real problem with the fighter would be its engines, since Continental was well behind the power curve with the units. The first two engines were received by Lockheed on 22 April 1942 but, rather amazingly, the powerplants had not been cleared for flight operation!

It was not until November 1942 that the aircraft was ready for flight testing, and on 11 November Joe Towle took the XP-49 aloft for a 35-minute flight over Burbank. On this initial hop, he reported that the prototype handled quite well. Lockheed had designed the aircraft so that two-thirds of its airframe components had some commonalty with the P-38 but its problems would stem from its engines, not the airframe.

In late November, the XP-49 was back at the experimental shop for the fitting of new XIV-1430-13/-15 powerplants, which had been rated at 1350 hp for take-off and 1600 hp at 25,000 ft. At this time, the early Royalin fuel tanks were replaced by P-38 self-sealing units, and a small second seat was added behind the pilot's position so that an engineer could accompany the pilot to monitor the aircraft's performance in flight.

By late December, the fighter was back in the air with Joe Towle at the controls, but the aircraft was developing assorted hydraulic problems, and on 1 January 1943 Towle skillfully brought the aircraft in for a crash landing at Muroc AAF Base

TOP Appearing at first glance to be a Lightning, the XP-49 incorporated P-38 parts and structure (modified fuselage pod and outer wing panels), but was otherwise a new design. Cancellation of the Model 522's original powerplants meant a healthy drop in projected top speed. Note how the aircraft's windscreen has been darkly tinted

CENTRE The rear view emphasises the larger fins and rudders of the XP-49. The extra canopy bracing for the pressurised cockpit is also visible, but it is unclear whether the pressurisation system was ever fitted to the aircraft

LEFT Handmade cowls that wrapped around the experimental Continentals were quite streamlined, and added to the XP-49's overall attractive lines

after experiencing hydraulic and electrical failures. One engine had been shut down in flight and the port main landing gear folded on touch-down. One can only imagine what flight engineer John Margwarth in the cramped rear position was thinking while all this was going on!

Repairs were undertaken, and at that time it was decided to enlarge the vertical tails by about eight inches. Back in the air, the XP-49 was delivered to Wright Field on 26 June 1943 – over two years behind schedule! At the Air Force's test base, only a few flights were made with the aircraft and, by then, the Continental engine programme was dead. One of the experimental engines failed during a test flight and, with no replacements, the XP-49 sat out rest of the war on the Wright ramp. During testing, it was determined that the XP-49's performance was actually inferior to the P-38J then in service.

The aircraft's final contribution to the development of aviation was rather ignominious. The XP-49 was attached to a hydraulic lift which raised the fighter into the air and then, with considerable force, dropped it back onto the concrete ramp. These tests were undertake to determine how many G forces could be handled by the gear before the aircraft's structure was damaged. As can be imagined, it did not take all that many drops before the XP-49 began exhibiting structural damage to the tail booms.

Somehow the aircraft survived this treatment to be displayed at the massive Wright Field Victory Air Display held soon after VJ-Day, but within weeks of this event, it had been stripped of useful parts – which were few – and then chopped up for scrap.

Photographed by William T Larkins on 13 October 1945 suspended in its drop rig at Wright Field, the XP-49 had by this late stage in its career received modern national markings – although the old-fashioned 'U. S. ARMY' titles were still carried under the wings. The XP-49 had a stronger gear than the P-38, and this was probably why the aircraft was selected for these unusual tests. As can be seen, the bottoms of the vertical fins have already been damaged by the drops. Failure of one of the Continentals soon after the prototype had been flown to Wright Field in late June 1943 meant that the XP-49's brief flying career was over by the end of the year

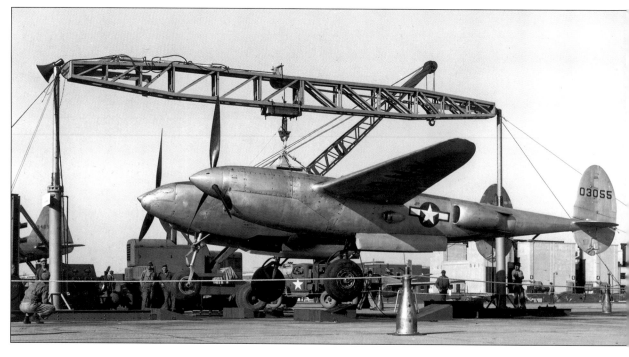

End of Rehearsal...

While the Axis rehearsed in China and Europe for this war, America's aircraft industry rehearsed too...expanded... and completed United States approved warplane orders for Britain and others in the front line of our defense.

In a dead serious dress rehearsal for today, we designed greater, tough-muscled warplanes, and geared for greater mass production. That's why American planes are this war's hard-boiled babies. That's why we are building more of them today, and will build yet more tomorrow. That's why air mastery inevitably will be with the United Nations.

For this mastery, Lockheed...first American mass producer for the Royal Air Force...builds P-38 "Lightning" interceptor pursuits and Hudson reconnaissance bombers. Lockheed Aircraft Corporation, Burbank, California

LOOK TO *Lockheed* FOR LEADERSHIP

Lockheed, *End of Rehearsal* . . . ,1942

Call it Lightning! ⚡
– SAY THE PILOTS

Nobody had time to name this Lockheed fighter plane when it was born. They just called it by a number, P-38.

Then the pilots sent it climbing over eight miles straight toward the stratosphere, up where even the highest-flying bombers couldn't go. They brought it screaming down out of the clouds like forked vengeance. They jammed down the throttle and it flew faster than any fighter ever flew before. They pressed the trigger-button and saw how *concentrated* fire-power from its cannon and machine guns could rip apart anything on wings—and there was only one name for it: *Lightning*.

So that's its name, a name it's earned from British and American pilots alike, a name to watch: Lockheed *Lightning*. Lockheed Aircraft Corporation...Vega Aircraft Corporation...Burbank, Calif.

for protection today, and
progress tomorrow, look to

Lockheed

FOR LEADERSHIP
Member Aircraft War Production Council, Inc.

Lockheed, *Call it Lightning! -SAY THE PILOTS*, 1943

Precision in name . . . precision in performance . . . Hughes Ball Bearings, Hughes Flexible Feed Chutes and Hughes Ammunition Boosters are all contributing their part in exacting efficiency to the brilliant achievements of our fastest fighters, and the responsibility for their perfection is a trust we accept with pride. Mastery of mass-production requiring such skill serves well as a pattern for the peace to come.

PRECISION

Armament Division

HUGHES AIRCRAFT CO.
A UNIT OF HUGHES TOOL COMPANY
HOLLYWOOD 38 CALIFORNIA
U.S.A.

Hughes Aircraft Co., *PRECISION*, 1944

BLACK PANTHER
WITH FISTS FULL O' FIRE!

From out of the blue, as if from nowhere, a formation of "Lightning" fighter planes streaks after the enemy. It's the Black Panther Squadron—America's "84th"—whose fighting insigne is the snarling panther with fists full of fire. True to their battle emblem, the men of the "84th" are daring and skillful fighters. Their planes are among the fastest and highest fliers of all. And at their command is the Fire-Power of long-range, fast-firing, heavy-hitting cannon! Here's a salute to the Black Panthers of the air—with good wishes, good luck, and "good hunting" in every mission against the enemy!

OFFICIAL INSIGNE
OF THE
84TH FIGHTER SQUADRON
U. S. ARMY AIR FORCES

Some of the heroic performances of America's fighter pilots in this war have been so amazing as to be almost unbelievable. There's the group of fliers, for example, who attacked and sank an enemy destroyer with nothing but the Fire-Power of their cannon-firing Lightnings . . . the Air Forces officer who shot down two enemy fighters with only three cannon shell . . . the pilot who exploded enemy locomotives, knocked out enemy tanks, smashed enemy installations—all with cannon Fire-Power . . . Such deeds stand as a fine tribute to the courage, the skill, the all-round fighting ability of the Army Air Forces personnel. We, at Oldsmobile, feel it has been a privilege to build thousands of the cannon these men are using in combat. In addition to *aerial* Fire-Power, we are also building several other types for both Army and Navy . . . cannon for tanks and tank destroyers, shell for tanks, artillery and naval guns. All to "Keep 'em Firing!"

OLDSMOBILE DIVISION OF GENERAL MOTORS
FIRE-POWER IS OUR BUSINESS

Oldsmobile, *BLACK PANTHER WITH FISTS FULL O' FIRE!*, 1944

GREMLIN
—on a Double-Eagle!

Here's to those eagle-riding "Gremlins" of the 339th Fighter Squadron, who fly into battle with this colorful insigne emblazoned upon their planes. With typical American humor, they call themselves "Gremlins," because they're so adept at making mischief . . . for the enemy. The double-eagle is symbolic, too, standing for the twin-bodied "Lightning" fighter planes these boys fly so skillfully. And that vicious looking spiked club represents the squadron's Fire-Power—the steel and high-explosive they throw from their cannon-firing planes . . . To every member of this famous group, on the ground as well as in the air, Oldsmobile pays respectful tribute!

We at Oldsmobile deem it a privilege to be producing Fire-Power for the fighting men who represent America on the battle-fronts today. We hope that our products have served them well, and will continue to do so until the last victorious shot is fired . . . Oldsmobile-built cannon for fighter planes, produced by the tens of thousands, have gone into action on every front in the world. These are *automatic* cannon, firing *high-explosive* shell. They're the same kind used by the flying "Gremlins" in running up their amazing scores. Oldsmobile also produces cannon for tanks and tank destroyers, high-explosive and armor-piercing shell for both Army and Navy.

FIRE-POWER IS OUR BUSINESS!

OLDSMOBILE DIVISION OF GENERAL MOTORS
≋ KEEP 'EM FIRING ≋

Oldsmobile, *GREMLIN – on a Double-Eagle!*, 1944

BOMB BUSTERS
—OF THE AAF

OFFICIAL INSIGNE
54TH FIGHTER SQUADRON
U. S. ARMY AIR FORCES

Designed at the very scene of battle, this insigne depicts the interception job the men of the 54th are trained to do . . . smashing enemy bombers before they can drop their bombs.

The shrill screech of an air raid alarm brings them out on the dead run. They vault into the cockpits of their Lightning fighter planes . . . taxi down the steel mesh runway . . . skyrocket toward the clouds in an almost vertical climb. The "Bomb Busters" are at it again! Swiftly, they gain altitude, fan out and search the sky for the enemy raiders. "There they are!" flashes the word. "Nine o'clock! Coming fast!" And the "Bomb Busters" sweep to attack, their cannon flashing fire . . . In the early days it was defense, keeping enemy bombers away from vital American installations. Today, the men of the 54th are on the offense, using their fire-power and fight-power to smash the enemy wherever he digs in. Keep it up, "Bomb Busters" . . . keep 'em on the run!

FIRE-POWER IS OUR BUSINESS

THE pilot in a fighter plane . . . the gunner in a tank turret . . . the loader in a gun crew . . . these are the men we're working for at Oldsmobile. These are the men we think about as we do our daily jobs, because we know that *their very lives* depend on us. It's our responsibility to put every bit of skill and care and "know how" we can muster into each Fire-Power product we build—into each automatic aircraft cannon for the Air Forces, each tank or tank destroyer cannon for the ground forces, each high-explosive or armor-piercing shell for the artillery and Navy. Thousands of these cannon and millions of these shell have already met the crucial test of combat on battle-fronts all over the world. More recent Oldsmobile products—including precision-built parts for Pratt and Whitney and Rolls Royce aircraft engines—will soon reach the stage of full volume production. It is our constant hope that these, too, will play a worthy share in the drive for final Victory!

HELP THE "BUSTERS" SOCK THE BOMBERS!

Show them you're behind them as they risk their lives for you. It's not only every American's patriotic duty to buy Bonds, it's good business, too. For every *three* dollars you put in today, you get back *four* after Victory.

BUY WAR BONDS!

OLDSMOBILE DIVISION OF GENERAL MOTORS
KEEP 'EM FIRING

Oldsmobile, *BOMB BUSTERS — OF THE AAF*, 1944

Finger-tip Control
MAKES THE *P-38* DOUBLY MANEUVERABLE!

The super-*P-38 Lightning* has been burning up the skies over enemy territory for months ... rolling up even more one-sided scores against Axis fighters.

This great fighter, made still greater with a sensational increase in speed, is *easier to handle* because it is now equipped with "finger-tip control" made possible by aileron boosters—a unique improvement developed by Lockheed engineers.

These boosters are actuated by the revolutionary Hycon "Stratopower" hydraulic pump, which also provides quicker response of other control surfaces. As a result, the plane is *twice as maneuverable* as previous models ... the pilot can aim and fire his guns more accurately and can out-fight many single engined ships, even in the thin air eight miles up in the stratosphere.

To help save American lives by speeding victory, we are forcing every facility to peak capacity in the production of Hycon "Stratopower" pumps. Until victory, all are reserved for fighting planes.

For Industry–When Victory Comes

When available to industry, the compact Hycon "Stratopower" pump, furnishing *variable volume up to 3000 pounds per square inch*, will perform many hydraulic jobs *better*.

Other Hycon Pumps and Valves are available today in the 3000-pound range for commercial applications to control or actuate dump truck lifts, giant presses, machine tools, remote control circuits and materials-handling mechanisms. They will test high-pressure apparatus; operate brakes, clutches and steering devices of heavy vehicles; and solve a wide variety of other hydraulic problems. Write for full information.

LET'S ALL BACK THE ATTACK—BUY MORE WAR BONDS

★ ★ **HYCON** ★ ★
REGISTERED TRADE MARK
Stratopower Pump

Patented — Manufactured only by The New York Air Brake Company

★

THE NEW YORK AIR BRAKE COMPANY
Hydraulic Division

420 LEXINGTON AVENUE, NEW YORK 17, N. Y.

HYCON, *Finger-tip Control MAKES THE P-38 DOUBLY MANEUVERABLE!*, 1944

Pay-off for Pearl Harbor!

Three years ago, the sneak attack on Pearl Harbor found America unprepared to defend its rights. Yet, even at that early date, Cadillac was in its third year of building aircraft engine parts for military use. Today we look hopefully forward to the time when this important contribution to America's air power will pay off in such a scene as that illustrated above.

For more than five years we have been working toward that end. Back in 1939, we started building precision parts for Allison—America's famous liquid-cooled aircraft engine—used to power such potent fighters as the Lightning, the Warhawk, the Mustang, the Airacobra and the new Kingcobra.

In addition to our work for Allison, which has included more than 57,000,000 man-hours of precision production—we assisted Army Ordnance Engineers in designing the M-5 Light Tank and the M-8 Howitzer motor carriage, and have produced them in quan-

tities. Both are powered by Cadillac engines, equipped with Hydra-Matic transmissions.

We are now building other weapons which utilize some of our Cadillac peacetime products. We can't talk about all of them yet—but we are confident they will prove significant additions to Allied armor.

Every Sunday Afternoon . . . GENERAL MOTORS SYMPHONY OF THE AIR—NBC Network

CADILLAC MOTOR CAR DIVISION GENERAL MOTORS CORPORATION

Cadillac, *Pay-off for Pearl Harbor*, 1944

CHAPTER 6

CHAIN LIGHTNING

WORLD WAR 2 STIRRED a frenzy of aircraft building in the United States, and many of these new aircraft were the epitome of form and function, while others were virtually useless and left their creators wondering why they were built in the first place. Unfortunately, the Lockheed XP-58 falls into the latter classification. The XP-58 had the misfortune to go through more redesign, re-engineering and re-classification than almost any other American wartime combat aircraft.

In 1939-40, when the British Aircraft Purchasing Commission was scouring America for combat aircraft that could 'aid the cause back home', they found that the Lockheed P-38 might be an ideal aircraft for long-range raids into Germany – something the short-range Spitfire could not do. The Air Corps, as previously related, was also interested in procuring just such a fighter, and Lockheed could see that a conflict could arise if production of aircraft for the 'home market' was disrupted while an order for fighters intended for Britain was negotiated.

Never an organisation to let an opportunity slip by, the Air Corps came up with an interesting agreement with Lockheed whereby the company would build – in exchange for the Air Corps granting them 'permission' to build Lightnings for the British – a prototype of an 'improved' P-38 at no cost to them. The agreement seemed to leave everyone happy except (eventually) the RAF, who discovered that their Model 322-61 was vastly inferior to the version being supplied to the Air Corps.

While all this was going on, work was progressing on the design of the Air Corps' 'free' aircraft. The concept for the improved Lightning was an interesting one, for it harked back to some rather dismal 1930s' aeronautical thinking. One of the big fears of the more excitable portion of the public during this 'anxious' decade had been expressed by lurid stories and illustrations carried in some of the more 'yellow journal' Sunday tabloids, which depicted vast fleets of enemy bombers in the 'next war' droning over major cities and flattening the same as they easily beat off attacks by ineffective interceptors.

Reasoning, at the time, figured that a massive, ultra-heavily armed interceptor could blast its way into the envisioned solid wall of bombers and break apart the formations by sheer fire power. It seems that little realistic thought was given to these future super bombers – along with the fact that Japan, Germany and other possibly hostile nations had little in the way of hardware that even approached this fictional high-altitude multi-engined fleet. Nevertheless, the concept of a 'super interceptor' remained an idea that intrigued the Air Corps, RAF and even the Luftwaffe – each organisation would eventually attempt to build their own version.

Back at Lockheed, the super Lightning programme was beginning to take form as an enlarged P-38 capable of wading into formations of enemy bombers, or escorting the Air Corps' own proposed strategic bombers and warding off attacks by hostile interceptors. A heavy armament was proposed for the new aircraft, which had taken the designation XP-58, and this would include a 20 mm cannon (soon increased to two) and two Browning air-cooled .50 cal machine guns in the nose, along with a similar weapon mounted in each tail boom to ward off attacks from the rear. A gunner would be seated behind the pilot with a remote control sight to fire the tail guns. At this time, the XP-58 was envisioned as being a bit larger than the P-38, and power was to come from two Continental IV-1430 engines, which had originally been designed in the late 1930s.

The Air Corps wanted some commonalty between the P-38 and XP-58, and requested that Lockheed use as many inter-changeable parts as possible. The Continental engine was, of course, an untried factor, but the company had a good reputation for building reliable powerplants for a wide variety of civilian and smaller military aircraft.

The only other American high-performance inline engine available in quantity was the Allison V-1710, so the prospect of a new military liquid-cooled engine was very welcome. Continental had sent the specifications of their IV-1430 to the Air Corps back in the latter part of 1939, but the Corps wanted more horsepower than the engine could produce (1600 hp), and the project was shelved. A proposal for a mated version of the engine (designated H-2860 and capable of 3200 hp) was also dropped because the Air Corps reasoned that the other, more established, engine companies would come up with similar engines in a shorter span of time. Both decisions were to prove incorrect and, with historical hindsight, it appears that both engines could have been successfully developed – especially with the lead times availaible if they had been ordered in 1939. With the emergence of the XP-58, the IV-1430 was dusted off and given a full development contract.

As Lockheed studied the Army requirement, it became apparent that the aircraft was beginning to grow at an alarming rate, and that more power would be needed. The first change in consideration of the XP-58's powerplants came in the middle of 1940 when the IV-1430s were dropped in favour of yet another new engine. This time the choice fell upon the Pratt & Whitney H-2600, which was a ponderous sleeve-valve (a type of engine favoured by Bristol in Britain) capable of 2200 hp.

This liquid-cooled giant fell by the wayside when Hap Arnold decided Pratt & Whitney should spend its time and resources developing the incredibly successful R-2800 series of air-cooled radials. Pratt & Whitney, in turn, proposed that Lockheed install the R-2800 in the XP-58, and although the airframe company thought this would be a workable solution, the Air Corps felt that a different engine was required.

There must have been a great deal of frustration in the Lockheed design department when the Wright R-2160 Tornado was selected for the new design (the project team numbered 187 by October 1941). Each engine change meant extensive interior changes to the aircraft's motor mounts, cowlings, interior plumbing and radiator set-up. The Tornado was an interesting engine, as it used six rows of seven cylinders each, was liquid-cooled and was capable of pumping out at least 2500 hp. The Air Corps appeared to be interested in the engine when, during November 1940, the service issued a contract for such engines to be supplied for the project.

The concept of extra power may have been a curse for the project, as the Air Corps began considering other items that could be tacked onto the fighter to take advantage of the power

From almost any angle, the XP-58 (Model 20-59) was a ponderous and unattractive aircraft. With Joe Towle at the controls, s/n 41-3670 was photographed on its way to Muroc AAF Base on 6 June 1944. The design did have possibilities as a nightfighter, but that role was undertaken by the Northrop P-61 Black Widow. After completing a limited flight test programme at Muroc, the aircraft was flown to Wright Field, in Ohio, where it rapidly became a mechanic's teaching aid before being scrapped. Note the huge cowlings needed to enclose the Allison V-3420 powerplants

and the proposed top speed of 450 mph. One of their first considerations was in the field of armament. The original armament was not all that heavy, so the Air Corps instructed Lockheed to install two turrets in the fuselage pod – one on top and one below – each with two .50 cals, while the nose section would take the very heavy armament of four 37 mm cannon, a burst from which would demolish any aircraft, be it a bomber or a fighter.

To adequately equip the cabin area for high-altitude fighting, the Air Corps now wanted the design to be pressurised. The weight of the extra weapons, ammunition, turrets, sighting mechanism and pressurisation system was making the overall weight of the XP-58 skyrocket.

As metal cutting started for the first aircraft, the second prototype was delayed so that additional fuel tanks could be designed which would increase the aircraft's range on internal fuel to just over 3000 miles. During the middle of 1941, Wright completed the first R-2160 and every bit of extra power that the elegant engine could produce would be needed, since the gross weight of the XP-58 had almost doubled, and was now approaching 36,000 lbs!

By 1942, it should have been clear to the new Army Air Force that the massive formations of advanced enemy bombers were just not going to appear. In fact, it seems that the Axis had virtually neglected the development of an efficient four-engined bomber that could cover vast distances and defend itself against enemy fighter attacks – certainly one of the real failings of the German and Japanese aircraft industries. The need for a porcine behemoth to wade into imagined bomber formations – without first being blown out of the sky itself – was

This detail view reveals the crew access hatch. The original XP-58 concept called for the cockpit to be pressurised, but the single prototype did not boast such a feature

just non-existent. However, both concerns in the XP-58 programme seemed to ignore this fact, but the AAF pulled a surprise late in 1942 when it suddenly, and radically, changed the XP-58's role – it would now be dedicated to ground attack!

Admittedly the four 37 mm cannon in the nose would be a powerful weapon in the ground attack mission, but the aircraft was extremely large (hence making a good target for all those enraged infantry men being strafed), and the plumbing system for the liquid-cooled engines was a nightmare that would have easily been destroyed or damaged by even light flak. However, the sheer size of the XP-58 meant that it could probably carry even larger weapons, and the AAF began investigating the possibility of installing a 75 mm cannon in the nose in place of the other weapons. In the low-level role, the pressurisation and turrets could be deleted but, because of extra armour and ammunition, the gross weight of the aircraft actually edged up a few more pounds.

The decision on the ground attack mission did not mean the programme was now going to 'enjoy a voyage through smoother waters'. On the contrary, the requirements and

With the left engine cowlings removed, the XP-58 performs a taxy test at Burbank. Note the 'face' temporarily painted on the nose. The prototype was never fitted with armament

problems were going to be more complex. Once again, the AAF changed missions, and the XP-58 went back to attacking any enemy aircraft that would sit still and let the lumbering twin-boom monster shoot it down.

To make matters worse, Wright was having trouble with the Tornado, and could not guarantee a delivery date to even match the slow development schedule of the aircraft, so the AAF called for yet another engine change. This time it was the ugly, and not particularly promising, Allison V-3420 which was chosen, the H-engine basically being created the simple joining of two of the company's trusty V-1710s.

It was back to the drawing board at Lockheed, where much cursing was probably being done by the accountants, who had been tallying the rising cost of the Army's 'free' fighter. New cowlings, tail booms, radiators and interior plumbing were once again designed and, finally, a fix was put on the project so that construction could rapidly begin. My mid-1943 it must have been evident to all concerned that the aircraft did not fit into a war that was being fought and won by fighters such as the Mustang, Thunderbolt and Lightning.

Dubbed 'Chain Lightning' by Lockheed employees, the XP-58, in a note of perhaps final irony, lifted into the air from Burbank on 6 June 1944 – the day of the Allied invasion of 'Fortress Europe'. By that time, the second XP-58 had been cancelled. Test pilot Joe Towle flew from Burbank to Muroc AAF Base, where around two dozen test flights were undertaken. Apparently, the XP-58 had decent handling qualities once in the air, but the complex engines and all the associated plumbing and systems made the Chain Lightning a maintenance nightmare. The aircraft was flown to Wright Field on 22 October 1944, but continued turbosupercharger 'torching' caused the XP-58 to be grounded. It was then used as a mechanic's teaching aid for a short time, before being scrapped.

Due to the many changes, the XP-58 programme became a monument to AAF mismanagement. After starting as a 'free' aircraft, the XP-58 would go on to cost taxpayers a stunning $2,345,107, and the aircraft served as an example of a concept that had gone very, very wrong.

CHAPTER ⎡7⎤ 'PIGGY-BACK'

During April 1943, aviation journalist Paul Pierce went for a ride with Lockheed's Jimmy Mattern in one of the company's 'piggy-back' P-38s. The following is what he wrote after his flight.

DON'T LET ANYBODY KID you about that fast, sturdy, flashing hunk of lethal airplane – it's *Lightning*! It's a big lightning, and I can prove it with facts and figures hitherto restricted by the Army. I can prove it also by telling you how it feels to ride as a passenger in one of the fastest, highest-flying, hardest-hitting and best-protected of all fighters.

The carefully guarded talk of my test pilot friends never quite satisfied my curiosity. The Lightnings flashing over my house every day only partly verified my guesses. It took a ride to find out the truth.

My pilot was Jimmy Mattern, 10,000-hour veteran of Army, barnstorming, mail flying and round-the-world hopping. Jimmy is one of Lockheed's test pilots, and a specialist on P-38s. He knows them – and loves to show what they'll do. That's why he's been assigned to the 'piggy-back' plane being used to demonstrate single-seat twin-engined fighter technique to commanding officers and flight leaders of Army fighter bases, who pass their observations on to their men. This new method of pilot training has already cut flying accidents from an index of 6.5 to a new low of 1.5 within two months.

Jimmy was standing on the flight line when I arrived at the airport. The overcast was almost solid over Burbank, with the ceiling between 3000 and 4000 feet, and a slight mist falling.

Jimmy went to the tower to check on the weather and I looked over the airplane I was to ride in. The P-38 has been described as 'three bullets on a knife' and that's close enough when it's in the air with gear retracted. The 'bullets' are the pod-shaped cockpit and the slim motor nacelles which fair back into the characteristic twin booms of the Lightning's tail. The knife is the razor-like wing that helps give this fighter its sensational performance. Halfway back are the bulging Prestone coolers, and clear aft are the twin, elliptical rudders, spaced by a long, thin horizontal flipper. Right now she stands on her three-legged landing gear, looking like a recalcitrant bronco, but ready to go. Her sister planes on the line have concentrated lead-tossing trouble sticking from their bullet-shaped noses, but our plane has had her guns removed to balance the weight of her passenger.

Piggie-Back I (note the misspelling) on the line at Burbank. The aircraft – USAAC s/n 41-7485 – was a P-38F-1-LO. Jimmy Mattern's displays in the aircraft were stunning, and included shutting down an engine on take-off and doing a roll into the dead engine! Although they had a 'cowboy' quality, the displays were well planned, and an excellent teaching aid for young P-38 trainees. At that time, there was a distinct lack of a good twin-engine trainer for the P-38 and Martin Marauder, both featuring very high wing loading. Mattern's displays helped cut accident rates, and his 'piggy-back' flights gave high ranking officers a good feel for the new fighter

Mattern came back with a 'go-ahead' and we climbed aboard. My quarters were not exactly palatial. The radio equipment had been removed from its place behind the pilot's seat and I squeezed in. I had my harness on and snapped the parachute to it, sliding the pack behind my back. I couldn't sit on it because my head was already banging the canopy, and I found I would have to remain stooped over for the entire flight. My seat was the main spar that runs clear through the ship, and the upholstering was a coat of paint. Mattern had his usual comfortable accommodations, with an inch or so of headroom when sitting up straight, but then the P-38 wasn't designed to accommodate deadheads.

Visibility from the cockpit was almost perfect and Jimmy taxied out like you'd drive your car. The tricycle gear makes ground handling easier. A quick run-up of engines, a crackle in Jimmy's earphones and a 'Roger' from him to the tower in return, and we were set for take-off. The canopy was closed and the engines revved up while Jimmy held the brakes on. There was a sudden rush, I clicked the stop-watch on my wrist, then looked up to see the airspeed reading 90 and winding right up. As it passed the 100 mph mark Jimmy pulled the wheel back an inch and we literally leaped into the air with the gear moaning up into the wells beneath us and the airspeed climbing frantically. A DC-3 started across our course at our altitude, but we were 1000 feet above it and a mile beyond it before I could tap my pilot on the shoulder and point. We finished one-quarter of our climbing circle of the airport and ran smack into a shredded, misty ceiling at 3500 feet.

Jimmy stuck the nose down to stay underneath while we both looked for a few tiny holes. We dove under the stuff and both saw it at once – a tiny patch of blue sky almost above us. Back came the wheel, down went my stomach and up went the Lightning through the hole. A few seconds and 15,000 feet later we were on top of a world of cotton and climbing into the sunlight.

There was more to come, however! The nose tilted higher until it was pointed up at 60° above the horizon and the rate of climb read over 5000 a minute! Jimmy half turned and said, 'A mile a minute straight up' and I could well believe it as I was lying almost on my back, with my shoulders on my parachute pack, and being shoved upstairs by some 2300 hp. Far from faltering in the climb, the ship picked up speed. Every few seconds Jimmy hauled back on the throttles a little more, explaining that 'the higher we go the more power we have with these turbos'.

At 10,000 feet we square away for cruising. As nearly as I could tell we were 20 miles from the field and two miles above it somewhere over Santa Monica, and the stop-watch said four minutes and 50 seconds. The engines were barely pulling and there was so little noise that we could talk freely, but we were gobbling up space at an appalling rate. Jimmy adjusted the prop pitch and the nose went down into a dive.

The sensitive altimeter started unwrapping and the airspeed went up to – well, let's say 'over 400'. Jimmy pulled back on the wheel gently, but in my hunched over position I found that I could not hold my head up. My mouth dropped open, my cheeks felt drawn and I felt five times as heavy in my seat as usual. The chandelle started at 5000 feet and we rolled out at the top above 12,000 feet.

Then came a demonstration. The right prop was feathered, the engine stopped and we cruised along on one engine. We climbed, did turns with and against the dead engine and finally peeled off after a fast medium bomber that slid by underneath us just above the clouds. Levelling off about three miles behind, Jimmy let the P-38 lose all the speed of the dive while he commented that the bomber was a pretty fast airplane. I agreed and he said, 'Watch this'. On one engine we took out in pursuit and went by the bomber like it was hanging on a sky hook. Our plane rolled away in a steep bank and I squashed down into my seat again as I wondered how a gunner in combat ever keeps track of the enemy. I was too busy holding my head to turn it around and look at the bomber.

The twin ribbons of Sepulveda Boulevard flashed past through a hole in the clouds, and I sang out our position to the pilot, who certainly did not need any help from me to know where he was. He knew all along and I had just found out. The wing went down, we swung back the three or four miles we had travelled in the last few seconds and slid down through a hole in a spiral dive. I caught a glimpse of the circular rainbow around our shadow on the shining white cumulus and then we were going through while I wondered about the traffic in the valley air below us. We broke out in the clear, dodged under a big patch of cloud (while I wondered about the hills that I knew were on the other side), and banked around for the airport. I made a suggestion about starting up the dead engine but Jimmy said 'Why bother, it flies fine on one'. I shut up and the pilot

Jimmy Mattern liked custom-made flight suits, and he is seen posing with one that boasted a bucking bronco insignia which matched the insignia on '485 when it was still finished in Olive Drab and Neutral Grey. When the fighter became due for an overhaul, it was stripped, polished and a red nose and tail stripes were added for a touch of colour. Gen Barney M Giles thought so much of Jimmy's flight displays as training aids that he recommended Mattern for a Civil Medal of Merit for his displays, which obviously eventually saved the lives of pilots and aircraft

concentrated on working off some excess airspeed without pulling back up into the clouds. We gobbled up the full width of the valley getting down to a slow 175 mph where we could put the wheels down. Polished aluminum panels on the camouflaged nacelles provided reassuring mirrors in which we could see the gear. Jimmy started the other engine, and we squared away for a landing.

The approach was easy and perfectly normal, with the flaps going down in the last three-quarters of a mile at about 1000 to 1500 feet. The glide is done power-off with the nose down only a little, a fairly high rate of sink, and with a quick flare-out just before touching down. Once the main wheels are on, the nose goes down and the tricycle gear rolls straight ahead. Jimmy made it look almost too easy, although he claims that any pilot can land this airplane. The airspeed said an even 100 when we touched, although the ship could be landed at 80 mph.

The stop watch said 20 minutes and six seconds, and we had really been places. I had a grin a mile wide and felt like Jimmie Doolittle although all I had done was take a routine airplane ride . . . and get myself a fine case of P-38 fever.

OPPOSITE TOP The 'piggy-back' came about through the flight department's use of the concept for testing. Milo Burcham watches as a flight engineer prepares equipment for a test flight. Note the absolute lack of room in the area that formerly housed radio equipment

OPPOSITE BELOW Jimmy brings the modified Lightning in close for the camera. Note how the passenger had to perch in a crouched position throughout the flight

GRAND CENTRAL 'PIGGY-BACK'

'Flying Tiger' ace R T Smith recalls a memorable 'piggy-back' flight

I had returned from China, and my duties with the American Volunteer Group, in the fall of 1942, was re-commissioned in the Army Air Force, and some months later took over command of the 337th Fighter Squadron – a P-38 training unit based at Grand Central Air Terminal in Glendale, California.

I was a Major by that time, had been married in June 1943, and my beautiful wife (Babs) often asked me to describe what it was like to fly a P-38. I finally told her that if she really wanted to know, I'd show her. I had one 'piggy-back' P-38 in the squadron, and an hour or so before dark one evening I suited her up in a pair of coveralls and stuffed her in that cramped space just behind the pilot's seat, much to the consternation of my line chief – a grizzled old master sergeant.

We took off and climbed to about 8000 feet, heading out toward the ocean, over Malibu, then across to Catalina, watching the sun set over the rim of the Pacific. I asked Babs if she wanted to do some aerobatics, and she nodded eagerly. I did a loop, and she was delighted, so I followed up with a couple of rolls, an Immelmann or two – the works. She enjoyed it immensely, and we headed back toward Glendale.

The lights of the city were coming on now, and they made for a beautiful sight on a clear evening – dark enough by the time we came down to require landing lights. Driving home that night she was chattering like a jay bird, and couldn't wait to tell her friends.

I'm afraid I bent the rules considerably on that occasion, and Babs was one of the very few females to fly in a P-38 except for the handful of WASPs who ferried them during the war from one place to another.

CHAPTER 8 'FORK-TAILED DEVIL'

BY LATE 1943 THE LIGHTNING had proven itself in a wide variety of missions – high-altitude fighter sweeps, bomber escort, medium altitude dogfights, ground attack missions and reconnaissance flights. The harsh conditions of North Africa had taken a heavy toll of Lightnings and USAAF pilots, but the aircraft had established itself as a valuable military tool, and new combat areas were rapidly opening up.

Back in Burbank, Lockheed was paying attention to reports from their field representatives and the USAAF. Hundreds of modifications were incorporated into the Lightning production line, while the design department came up with new variants. Reports from the combat fronts had told of power falling off above 25,000 ft. Automatic oil radiator flaps were fitted to the new P-38H (226 P-38H-1-LO variants constructed) that not only enabled the Allison V-1710-89/91 powerplants, with a take-off rating of 1425 hp, to run cooler, but let the pilot keep military power on above 25,000 ft, where 1240 hp per engine could be achieved. The P-38H-5-LO (375 built) also had the more power-ful B-33 turbosuperchargers installed in the booms.

Major improvements were introduced with the P-38J. One of the key identifying features of the earlier Lightnings was the elegant swept-back 'shark' intake behind and below the spinner, which gave the Allison engine installation an extremely stream-lined appearance. However, such an arrangement offered inad-equate cooling for the engines once performance demands on the Lightning increased.

A P-38E (s/n 41-1983) had been modified at the factory to incorporate larger radiators and much larger scoops under the spinners. This did detract from streamlining but, at the same time, offered an impressive increase in power. With the larger radiator area and new Prestone coolant scoops mounted on the booms, the Allisons could operate more efficiently. Testing with the P-38E had proven the installation more than satisfactory, and the modification was incorporated into the new P-38H production run. The P-38J (Model 422-81-14) kept the same engine installation as the P-38H, but the increased cooling meant that power at 27,000 ft would go from 1240 to 1425 hp.

A complete Allison QEC is carefully lowered into position for installation on a P-38L's cantilever motor mounts. Having the engine, accessories and cowling formers preassembled for installation saved a great deal of time on the production line. This view illustrates the new intercooler intakes to advantage

OPPOSITE TOP P-38J-10-LO USAAF s/n 42-68040 displays the new natural metal finish that replaced the camouflage as worn by the Lightning on the left. The elimination of camouflage paint saved man-hours at the factory, but the harsh salt-laden climate of the Pacific took a quick toll on the bare aluminum finish. However, the Lightning was viewed by the AAF as an expendable item, since they estimated that individual aircraft would not last more than 500 flying hours in the frontline

LEFT Even though women had made major inroads on the production line, less progress was made in Lockheed's design offices, since employment was often based on a college degree in engineering. This view of a solitary female design engineer in an office otherwise dominated by men gives some idea of the disparity

ABOVE This photograph of the Lockheed flightline during late 1944 reveals rows of natural-metal Vega-built B-17Gs and Lightnings, accompanied by a few camouflaged US Navy PV-2 Harpoons

War emergency power selection at that altitude would take engine power to 1600 hp for a few minutes. The Model 422-81-14 was built in large numbers – 10 P-38J-1-LOs, 210 P-38J-5s and 790 P-38J-20s. Each block variant had improvements, including the addition of two 55 US gallon fuel cells in the space previously occupied by the intercoolers (J-5), which increased internal fuel to 410 US gallons. Flat armour glass windshields were added to the J-10, along with other minor improvements.

The Model 422-81-22 production was divided into two main batches – the P-38J-15-LO (1400 built) had an updated electrical system, while the J-20 (350 built) had new turbosupercharger regulators. The Model 422-81-23 block consisted of 210 P-38J-25s that had dive flaps located under the wing that were electrically-powered, and they were also fitted with ailerons that had power boost systems (dive flaps would also be built as kits for installation on earlier aircraft 'in the field').

The P-38L (Model 422-87-23) was the final production version of the Lightning, and it was built in two blocks. Power came from V-1710-111/-113 Allisons, with a war emergency rating of 1600 hp at 28,700 ft and a military rating of 1475 hp

LEFT This camouflaged P-38J wears Chinese Nationalist markings, and is seen on the Burbank flightline. Lightnings were not widely used by the Allies, but small numbers were supplied to China, France and Italy (after the latter country's surrender to the Allies in September 1943)

RIGHT A worker adjusts the nose gear on a P-38J before the fighter is rolled out of the assembly building

BELOW This P-38J was photographed taxying out for a test flight toting seven 4.5-inch High Velocity Aerial Rockets under each wing. Numerous rocket configurations were tested by both the AAF and Lockheed for the P-38

at 30,000 ft. Lockheed built 1290 L-1-LOs, which were similar to the J-25-LO. A stunning 2520 L-5-LOs were also constructed, and these had submerged fuel pumps and provisions for under-wing rocket launchers, as well as strengthened centre section pylons for 2000-lb bombs. With production rising at Lockheed, a license-building agreement was undertaken with Vultee in Nashville, Tennessee, to build P-38s, starting with a batch of 2000 P-38L-5-VNs, but production delays saw just 113 completed by VJ-Day, and the remainder swiftly cancelled.

With the P-38L, the General Electric B-33 turbosuperchargers were mounted in the top of each forward boom at station 207, and were attached to the centre section rear shear beam. Air entering the system through scoops mounted on the outboard side of each boom below the wing was rammed into the impeller section of the turbosupercharger, where it was compressed. The compressed air then passed through a duct to the intercooler, and then to the carburretor.

The air induction system controlled the intake, flow and temperature of the air from the intake scoops to the carburet-

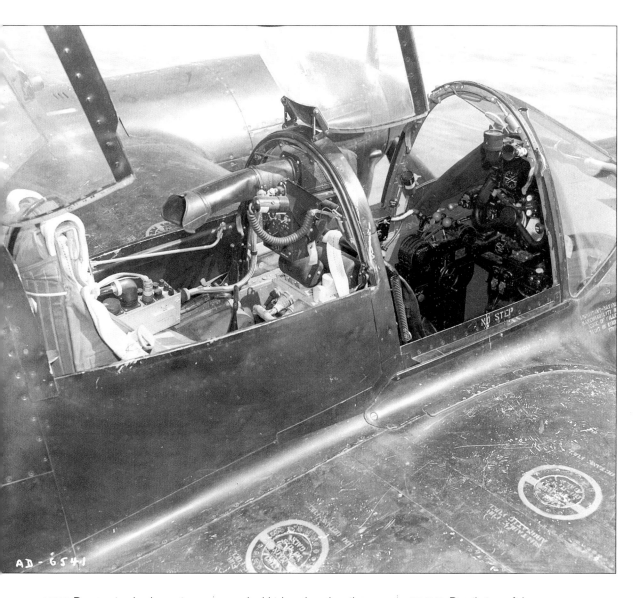

AD-6541

LEFT Due to size, load-carrying ability and twin engines, the Lightning was chosen for conversion into an interim night-fighter. Given the designation P-38M, all converted aircraft had been originally built as P-38Ls. Modifications included the installation of the radar unit in a large pod under the forward nose, blast muzzles on the weapons to prevent the pilot's night vision from being ruined, and a second seat and raised bubble hood for the radar operator, sat behind the pilot. The radar operator (r/o) sat perched higher than the pilot, with the viewing port for the radar screen projecting directly into his face. Finally, all P-38Ms were given a gloss black finish for their nocturnal role

ABOVE Detail view of the two positions in the P-38M. The nightfighter conversions were carried out at the Dallas, Texas, modification facility

tors. A closed system of ducts, starting with the boom-mounted intake scoops, controlled and routed the air flow.

From the scoops, the air went through the air filter (if in operation) through the compressor of the supercharger, and through pressure-tight ducts to the intercooler. The intercooler was of the core type, and was equipped with electrically-operated flaps. Compressed hot air from the turbosupercharger passed around the tubes of the cooling element and was cooled sufficiently to make it suitable for engine operation. From the intercooler, the air passed by pressure-tight ducts to the carburettor.

An auxiliary system of scoops and ducts was provided to conduct cooling air to various sections of the engine. Air was directed to the spark plugs, magnetos, distributors and to the cap baffles of the turbosupercharger. This cooling air remained in a free state, and escaped to the outside atmosphere after use.

Exhaust manifolds from the cylinder banks converged in a 'Y' aft of each engine, and a shrouded tail pipe carried exhaust gases from that point to the supercharger nozzle box. Gases passed through the supercharger and out the wastegate, after driving the turbine bucket wheel. The latter was mounted at opposite ends to the compressor impeller on the same shaft.

The empennage of the P-38L consisted of two empennage booms, two vertical stabilisers, two rudders and tabs, one horizontal stabiliser and one elevator and tab. The horizontal stabiliser tips were interchangeable, right and left, and were attached to the outboard sides of the empennage booms. The elevator was made of one panel and attached to the horizontal stabiliser by ball-bearing hinges. The operating cables actuated a torque tube in each empennage boom. The torque tubes were fastened to the elevator by screws.

The elevator tab was located on the centre line of the P-38, in the trailing edge of the elevator. It was attached to the elevator by a hinge fitted with a corrosion-resistant steel hinge pin, and was connected to the actuating unit in the horizontal stabiliser by a push-pull tube. A clip at the left end of the elevator secured the tab hinge pin. The inboard ends of the elevator torque tubes were carried in bearings on the stabiliser rear spar. The torque tube balance arm, attached to the outboard end of the tube by two taper pins, contained a bearing that slipped over a pin to the empennage boom. The arms extended forward, and to them were fastened the control cables and the balance weights.

The rudders were constructed in two sections, upper and lower, and were interchangeable, right and left. Rudders were attached to the vertical stabiliser by ball-bearing hinges, and to the torque tubes and to each other by screws. A counterbalance extended forward of the hinge line of each section. The rudder tab was attached to its rudder by a hinge, with a corrosion-resistant steel hinge pin, and was connected to the actuating unit by a push-pull tube. A clip on the rudder at the lower end of the upper rudder secured the hinge pin.

OPPOSITE TOP Since production was scattered around the Lockheed Air Terminal, quite a bit of aircraft moving took place at night, as can be seen by these P-38Ls being towed down a street to the Lockheed Air Terminal from the B-1 facility during March 1945

LEFT Approximately two days' worth of P-38L output is seen in Production Flight Test Building 304. At this point, aircraft received final work before flight testing. Note that the armament has been fitted, along with the underwing drop tanks

The rudder torque tubes, bearings, brackets and arms were assembled as units, and were attached to the vertical stabilisers by bolts. The control arm projected outboard from each tube, and connected by a push-pull tube to the walking beams in the boom. The empennage boom consisted of two parts, forward and aft, which were joined at boom station 430. The empennage boom formed a tail cone to the aft beam, the tail cone fairing to a trailing edge flush with the horizontal stabiliser tip, and with the elevator when it was in neutral position. The horizontal stabilizer tip was attached to both fore and aft sections.

The forward empennage boom supported the horizontal and vertical stabilisers, and housed the actuating linkage of the rudder and elevator controls. Access was provided through the lower outboard fillet.

The vertical stabilisers were constructed in upper and lower sections, interchangeable right and left. In the upper sections were the rudder tab actuating units, a navigation light showing on the outboard side only, one elevator control pulley and two rudder tab control pulleys. Each lower section carried one elevator control pulley and a steel shoe to protect the lower tip against damage in the event of a tail-down landing. The rudder hinge brackets and the rudder torque tubes were attached to the rear spars.

Preformed tinned or galvanised aircraft cable (Spec AN-RR-CRS) was used throughout the surface control system. Terminals were swaged on all cable ends except those in the aileron booster and the fly carriages, where bushings were centred in eyes bound by micropress oval sleeves. Sealed bearing anti-friction pulleys were used exclusively. Cables were stretched before installation, and were coated with a rust-preventive compound.

The elevator and rudders were each fitted with a trim tab actuated by a revolving drum on an acme-threaded push-pull

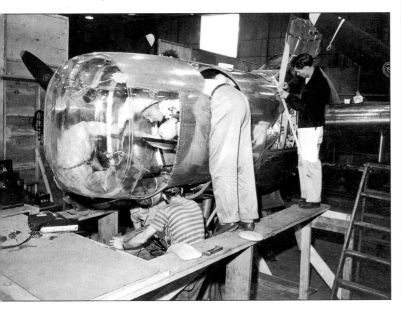

OPPOSITE Three rows of P-38Ls are seen in final stages of completion. Note the protective covers applied to the tops of the wings

LEFT With the success of the 'Droop Snoot' conversions carried out in Ireland, Lockheed built an unspecified number of Pathfinder conversions at Burbank. These aircraft featured a greatly extended nose, housing an AN/APS-15 radar

rod. The trim tabs were manually adjusted in the cockpit by hand cranks geared to operating drums, which were connected by cables to the actuating drums. Ailerons were equipped with fixed trim tabs.

The control column was a hollow inverted L-shaped member consisting of aluminum alloy tubing. It was mounted on the right-hand side of the fuselage on two ball bearings located below the floor of the cockpit, and between the outer skin and wheel well web.

The aileron control wheel was mounted at the upper extremity of the 'L', and turned approximately 144° each way from neutral when full throw of the ailerons was effected. Aileron throw was limited by piston travel in the booster-actuating cylinder. The aileron cable was secured to a drum keyed on the control wheel shaft, whence it was carried over pulleys at the angle of the 'L' downward to a second set of pulleys located at the centre line of the column pivot bearings, where the two ends of the cable left the column.

The lower extremity of the control column contained the bearings to which were attached the elevator control cables. Threaded adjustable stops limiting the fore-and-aft movement of the column were located below the floor, and could be reached through the wheel well.

In addition to the flight controls, the control column carried the gun camera switch box, the gunsight switch box and a fluorescent light bulb for the instrument panel. The control wheel had a push button switch for a bomb release, and a trigger switch for cannon and machine guns on the right hand grip, a microphone switch on the right hand spoke of the wheel and a dive flap switch on the left hand spoke. An engine operation placard was mounted on the aft side of the control column at the angle of the 'L'.

The ends of the cables from the control column were fastened by turnbuckles to both ends of a second cable which ran aft to pulleys under the main beam, up through holes in the

LEFT P-38J-15-LO USAAF s/n 44-23139 is seen on the Burbank ramp after modification to Pathfinder configuration. The seat for the radar operator was located behind the radar unit, and was defined by the window cut into the former armament section

ABOVE 'Kelly' Johnson and Milo Burcham go over the operation of the new dive flaps fitted to the P-38

RIGHT Gen Hap Arnold (right) is seen during one of his numerous inspection tours at Lockheed conferring with company president, Robert Gross (centre), as new P-38Ls are prepared for flight testing behind them

BELOW A near-complete P-38L is raised from the production line, showing such detail as the turbosuperchargers, and their stainless steel shrouds, to advantage

ABOVE This billboard display at Lockheed used stars to symbolise femployees from the plant that had gone into the military

LEFT Lockheed employees load ammunition into the spacious gun bays of P-38J-25-LO USAAF s/n 44-23560

lower beam cap and around the larger circumference of a reduction drum mounted inside the main beam. From this point outboard to each aileron the right and left hand systems were independent, and either side could be disabled without affecting the other.

Cables to the ailerons were secured around the smaller circumference of the drum. To the left, one passed over and under pulleys mounted at the centre line of the aeroplane through a fairlead at station 110, near the rear face of the outer panel main beam, and were secured to the quadrant of the aileron booster unit. To the right aileron, the lower cable passed over a pulley at station 15, and from this point outboard the system was similar to that on the left hand side.

One pair of cables led forward from the lower end of the control column, around pulleys at fuselage station 95, and aft to pulleys under the main beam. Another pair of cables travelled aft to a similar set of pulleys in the same location. All four cables entered the beam and passed over pulleys near the lower beam cap. An UP cable and a DOWN cable travelled outboard through the beach each way to pulleys near wing station 89, where they turned aft into the booms, travelling along the inboard side of each forward boom between the skin and the wheel well web. Aft of the wheel well the cables were in the upper portion of the boom.

At boom station 402, the UP cable went down into the lower vertical stabiliser, around a pulley and up to the lower eye of the elevator balance arm, and the DOWN cable went up over a pulley in the upper vertical stabiliser, and down to the upper eye of the same balance arm, whose travel was limited by adjustable stops.

An elevator tab control unit was mounted in the side control stand. Cables from this unit went down around pulleys under the floor, aft up into the main beams, outboard on the left hand side to wing station 89, aft through the boom in a manner similar to the elevator cables, diagonally inboard through the horizontal stabiliser, and around the tab actuating drum on the centre line of the aeroplane.

The hydraulic system operated the landing gear, wing flaps, coolant radiator, exit flaps and the aileron boosters. Hydraulic pressure was supplied by two engine-driven variable volume pumps for an operating pressure of 1350 psi. An auxiliary hand pump with a reserve supply of fluid provided for the operation of all landing gear and wing flaps should the engine-driven pumps fail.

An emergency hydraulic system, with separate lines and a reservoir, and using the auxiliary hand pump for a pressure source, provided a means of extending the landing gear in case the main hydraulic system failed. The system was connected by independent lines to the landing gear UP locks. The UP locks had separate chambers for the emergency system. When the pressure in these chambers built up to approximately 250 psi,

96823-R

P-38L-5-LO

S SER. 44-25413

00 LBS.

ANE WITH
IF NOT AVAIL-
WILL BE
ENCY
AROMATICS

SH

ONLY

the UP lock pins were withdrawn from the axles. Fluid then flowed from the UP lock to the shuttle valves on the landing gear actuating cylinders. As fluid forced these shuttle valves over, the ports to the main hydraulic system were closed off and the fluid flowed into the cylinder, extending the gear.

The emergency system did not open the wheel well doors. However, when the landing gear lever was in the DOWN position, the weight of the wheels would force the doors open.

An aileron booster system used the main system hydraulic pressure to supplement the pilot's pressure on the control column. Operation was such that the pilot maintained the feel of the control, yet was able through servo action to produce a greater force at the ailerons.

There was an aileron booster unit installed in each wing. Each unit consisted of a quadrant and bellcrank assembly, a control valve, an actuator cylinder assembly and a bypass control assembly. The bypass control cylinders automatically bypassed the hydraulic fluid through the actuating cylinder when hydraulic pressure was lost. The booster units were connected to the ailerons by push-pull tubes.

With hydraulic pressure ON, the aileron booster transmited servo action as long as the pilot rotated the control wheel to exert one-sixth of the aileron load. An extreme turn of the wheel (about 144°) would raise one aileron 25° and lower the other 20°. This differential action was achieved by the pivoting position of the push-pull rods on the booster bellcrank. Without hydraulic pressure, the ailerons operated in the normal manner.

The wing and centre section flaps were interconnected, and operated together. They were actuated by a hydraulic motor, which drove them through a mechanical linkage. The flaps were attached at each end to carriages that rolled in tracks built into the wing structure. The carriages were linked by cables to push-pull tubes, travelling in roller brackets on the rear face of the rear shear beam. The push-pull tubes were actuated by long screws, driven by a hydraulic motor housed under a removable panel at the aft end of the fuselage.

The flaps had three automatic positions, UP, DOWN and MANEUVERING. The flaps could also be used in any position between UP and DOWN by holding the cockpit control handle in the UP or DOWN position until the desired amount of flap was reached, then returning the handle to the CLOSED position. The flap control system consisted of a four-way selector valve, a piston-type hydraulic drive motor, and a travel limit valve. The motor was mounted on the flap drive gearbox, which was bolted to the centre section aft shear beam.

The new variants of the Lightnings were soon on their way to all corners of the globe, replacing earlier Lightnings, and giving the USAAF a fighter that was greatly feared by the enemy. Indeed, so feared that Luftwaffe pilots dubbed the P-38 'the Fork-tailed Devil'.

ABOVE An end to an American era – Lockheed workers celebrate the announcement of the unconditional Japanese surrender. Most of these workers would soon be laid off as the government made massive defence contract cancellations

OPPOSITE A Lockheed worker completes hydraulic system detail work on a P-38L

CHAPTER 9 | # MILO AND YIPPEE

ON 20 OCTOBER 1945 Lockheed chief test pilot Milo Burcham strapped into the cockpit of YP-80 s/n 44-83035, which was the third example of the radical new jet fighter built for the Army Air Force as part of an order for 13 service and evaluation aircraft. After performing a complete cockpit check, Milo fired up the General Electric I-40 and headed for the active. With one final check and clearance from the tower, Milo stood on the brakes and brought the engine up to full power. Releasing the brakes, the jet initially accelerated slowly down the Burbank runway but rapidly began to increase speed. Lifting the aircraft smoothly off the runway, Milo brought up the gear but the engine flamed out – the fuel pump had failed and there was no back-up unit. With no where to go, and too low to parachute, the test pilot turned the stricken fighter away from a populated area and crashed into a gravel pit – he died upon impact.

The loss of the popular Burcham was a blow to the company. Born in Newcastle, Indiana, Burcham considered himself a Californian by adoption, and attended Whittier High School and Whittier College in southern California. Fascinated by flight, and adept with all things mechanical, Milo invented a home burglar alarm and sold the device to pay for his first flying lessons. Obtaining his pilot's license in 1928, the young aviator soon developed a flare for aerobatics and air racing, and was in demand for airshow work all across the country. Despite the gasps he drew from admiring crowds, Burcham made sure that every manoeuvre was carefully thought out, and that his aircraft was checked to the smallest detail.

In 1937 Milo joined Lockheed and was put to work as a ferry pilot. Two years later he was sent to Britain and put in charge of flight testing at the company's Liverpool division. Subsequently recalled to Burbank, his thoroughness and skill as a pilot brought about his assignment to engineering flight testing, where he began flying YP-38s.

Promotion came rapidly and, as chief test pilot, Burcham was in charge of 85 fellow test pilots at Burbank. His low-key manner hid an amazing skill for flying – especially the P-38. A fellow test pilot said, 'When he was alone over the desert, I've

Milo Burcham *(left)* arrives on 'Smokey' at the Lockheed guard gate on Hollywood Way, followed by fellow test pilot Joe Towle

Milo Burcham with *YIPPEE* on the Lockheed ramp. Fully combat-equipped, the aircraft was finished in the special bright red scheme to honour the 5000th Lightning built at Burbank. After ceremonies were completed, the paint was stripped and normal USAAF markings applied

seen him do some of the damndest things a man ever did with an airplane – stunts even a bird would not try'.

Milo always insisted on doing the most hazardous testing himself. It was his desire to help young Army Air Force pilots master the Lightning that prompted development of a special course of P-38 instruction that he carried out during the summer of 1945 at Fourth Air Force bases up and down the west coast. He showed young pilots manoeuvres they thought impossible with the P-38 – especially those that Milo performed with one engine out at low altitude and slow speeds.

Milo used to drive his battered old Ford to stables where he kept horses for himself, his wife and two sons. From the stables he would ride 'Smokey' the two-and-a-half miles to Lockheed's Pilot House, where he would tether the horse and complete the journey on a bicycle. Indeed, one of the few injuries the test pilot would receive was when 'Smokey' slipped on loose gravel and fell on his master.

Burcham often took long walks at midnight, pondering some strange problem of flight he had encountered during the day. He was one of the first pilots to peer over the scientific abyss of compressibility – to enter that area of high speed in the air where odd behaviour of supposedly immutable laws of physics confounded aviation's ablest minds. His test dives helped engineers create solutions to baffling aerodynamic problems.

A visit to the Mayo Clinic to study reactions to high

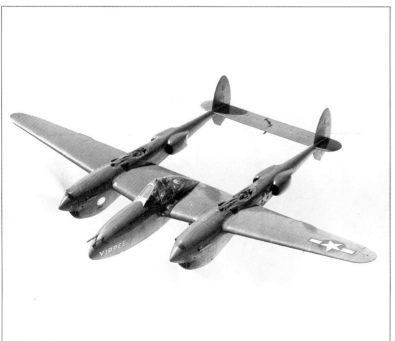

ABOVE Milo Burcham developed a special course to show young USAAF pilots that the P-38 could be handled at low altitude and slow speed with an engine out, and his dramatic flight demonstrations undoubtedly saved the lives of many fledgling fighter pilots. Milo brings *Yippee* in close to the camera-ship with the left shut down, but not feathered

LEFT *YIPPEE* displays its red finish over a fog bank near Burbank

altitude flying convinced Burcham that decompression of pilots who fly above 30,000 ft was not only desirable but absolutely necessary. As a result, Lockheed installed decompression equipment for its test pilots.

From his well-equipped home workshop, Burcham produced several instruments and devices which company engineers made standard equipment for the new Constellation. They were developed out of work to answer specific problems he met while conducting engineering test flights of the four-engined transport. Two of his better-known inventions included a visual oxygen meter that enabled a pilot to keep a closer check of his oxygen supply at high altitudes, and a device that permitted delivery of mail from a aeroplane in flight!

Milo Burcham will always to associated with the brilliant red P-38J-20-LO that carried the exclamation *YIPPEE* under the wings. This was the 5000th Lightning built by Lockheed, and it was given the special paint scheme to honour that event. Milo put on a very convincing display for employees in this aircraft on 17 May 1944 when a series of stunning photographs was taken by Erik Miller.

On 24 October 1945 Milo Burcham was buried at Forest Lawn Memorial Park as Lightnings roared overhead – one group forming a cross and the other a V for victory symbol. The first group (forming the cross) came from Van Nuys Airport, and was led by Maj S A Long, whilst the second formation had flown out of Ontario AAF Base, with Maj M Millard in the lead. Both officers were veterans of the Aleutian campaign. After overflying the cemetery, the P-38s continued over the Burbank factory and Air Terminal, before returning to their bases.

Breaking away from the camera, Milo reveals the huge *YIPPEE* titling under the fighter's wings

CHAPTER ☐10 PHOTO FIGHTERS

ALTHOUGH THE FAMILIAR shape of the P-38 is easily recognised and admired by aviation enthusiasts, it is not commonly known that more than one in eight Lightnings built were finished with cameras in place of weapons. Indeed, the 'photo fighter' Lightning became one of the USAAF's most effective reconnaissance tools (by comparison, the USAAF took on fewer than 500 North American Aviation F-6 Mustangs). From being one of the top fighter aircraft of World War 2, the Lightning went on to become an outstanding intelligence gatherer.

As the war evolved in Europe, and America was drawn closer to the conflict, the British and French realised that the speed at which the German *Blitzkrieg* moved made up-to-date intelligence vital. The most efficacious method of intelligence gathering was, of course, by aircraft. However, most reconnaissance (or observation, as the mission was usually classified during that time period) aircraft were slow and lumbering affairs that usually offered stable platforms for cameras, but little else. To send such machines into areas where Messerschmitt fighters enjoyed air superiority was suicidal, but commanders had little choice, hoping that the aircraft could find some protection in cloud cover, and return with the desired results.

Needless to say, many of these aircraft simply did not return, and the ones that did come back often had to abort their mission because of heavy anti-aircraft fire, or because approaching fighters had caused them to turn back prematurely.

Obviously, some form of specialised photo reconnaissance aircraft was needed in the worst way. After France was overrun and the British Expeditionary Force driven from Dunkirk in defeat, it became absolutely essential to get photographs of what was going on in occupied Europe. Accordingly, the RAF fitted cameras to a variety of fighters and bombers, and sent them over enemy territory – usually alone and unescorted. Sometimes the aircraft returned with important photos, whilst on other occasions they didn't. Photo reconnaissance had come a long way since World War 1, when primitive biplanes droned over the trenches as the observer attempted to take photos with his bulky aerial camera. It was a science that was rapidly evolv-

ing and the Allies were in a desperate race to catch up, create an efficient method of gathering photos and, just as importantly, create a system of developing, interpreting and dispersing the information gathered by the aircraft, and their brave crews.

Since America and its Allies had such a great need for new aircraft, orders were being placed even before the YP-38 service test aircraft had flown and, on 30 August 1940, the Air Corps placed a contract for 410 P-38s. Tthis order was to have significance since it specified that some of the aircraft would be built as F-4, F-4A, F-5 and F-5A photo reconnaissance variants.

The F-4/F-5 variant of the Lightning was a relatively simple modification to the airframe. The guns and associated armament accessories were removed and camera mounts and clear vision windows installed, along with needed wiring and controls for the pilot. The first photo Lightnings had their distinctive nose profile changed only slightly to accommodate the cameras, but later variants had wildly different noses that were a complete departure from the Lightning's smoothly flowing fighter nose. However, these variants had two things in common – they were desperately needed, and were extremely efficient.

Lockheed and the Air Corps reasoned that the photo-recon

From 'D-Day minus seven' until 'D-Day plus 14', photo Lightnings took over 3,000,000 aerial photographs of the Normandy coast, and associated areas. Gen Dwight Eisenhower credited the F-5s with furnishing him with the most valuable information on invasion progress during that period. Gen Hap Arnold also commented, 'Our photo reconnaissance pilots are instructed to fly on the theory that fighter planes win battles while camera planes win wars'. This warmly-dressed F-5A pilot watches while camera gear is installed in the spacious nose compartment that once held weapons and ammunition. This particular aircraft is finished in Haze Paint

ABOVE The nose of a P-38 modified to F-4 configuration (faired over gun ports are visible on the original print), showing two vertical cameras. The F-4 nose could carry four cameras, the pilot operating their controls via switch boxes. The first F-4s were retained for training and designated RF-4-1-LO, the 'R' indicating restricted (non-combat) use only

LEFT This pilot is dressed in lightweight flight gear, and he is seen helping a crewman install a film pack in his Olive Drab and Neutral Grey F-5A. The camera's large upward-opening doors afforded excellent access. Equipped with up to five cameras, the aircraft boasted seven ports in its nose fairing to give extensive coverage. F-5s could penetrate enemy areas at either high or low altitude usually at full power, since speed was the key to survival

RIGHT An F-5 has equipment installed in its camera bay on the Burbank ramp. This view shows three of the ports to advantage, along with the additional camera access door in the nose. Note the position of the radio antenna, and the fact this Lightning is also finished in Haze Paint

BELOW The Lightning was the most numerous of all American wartime photo fighters, with over 1400 F-4s and F-5s accepted by the Air Force. Lockheed modified P-38Es on the production line into F-4-1-LOs, fitted with the 1150 hp Allison V-1710-21/29 powerplants. Quickly pressed into service, F-4s went into action in November 1942 with the 5th PRS in North Africa. This particular aircraft, parked on the Burbank ramp, is finished in the original Haze scheme

This Haze-painted F-5 has its external tanks topped off prior to conducting a test flight from Burbank

variants could dispense with their armament and rely on high altitude and high speed for safety. This idea had some merit, but as the enemy began developing more advanced fighters, the life of a photo-recon pilot steadily became more fraught with danger. It was an unglamorous mission that received little publicity in comparison with the sleek twin-boom fighters that were flashing through swarms of German and Japanese aircraft.

Much of the photo modification work was done at depot level, the aircraft leaving the Burbank line as fighters and being flown to facilities such as the one in Dallas, Texas, where armament was removed and necessary photo modifications installed. This way, the main production lines were not slowed down by the need to build different variants at the same time.

The photo Lightnings made their first combat appearance in North Africa, where they were operated by the 5th and 12th Photographic Reconnaissance Squadrons (PRS) from November 1942. Flying F-4s, these brave pilots flew from harsh and primitive strips against an enemy who had yet to suffer the wounds of defeat. It was a hazardous task, and losses were not infrequent, but the photo Lightnings brought back important results that were essential to the Allied war effort. As newer aircraft became available, the two units transitioned to the F-5, and were joined by two squadrons of the 3rd Photographic Reconnaissance Group (PRG).

The importance of the photo Lightning was such that some fighters were converted to the photo-recon role in the field, and these aircraft often retained a modicum of armament – usually two or three .50 cals, that could pose a nasty surprise for the enemy, especially when he thought that he was attacking an unarmed 'recon bird'. The 154th PRS was one such unit, taking P-38Fs and converting the fighters to photo mounts in the harsh North African environment.

F-4s and F-5s also operated in other unpleasant parts of the globe. The 28th Composite Group flew F-4s in Alaska from 1942, operating over the Aleutians, where enemy floatplane fighters attempted to control the skies over the occupied islands – the only American territory occupied by the enemy during the war. It was a difficult operating environment, with neither the enemy nor nature giving any quarter, and losses were high.

The 8th PRS, with its distinctive 'Eight-Ball' insignia, started operating in New Guinea, where the powerful Lightnings quite often outran Japanese fighters to bring home photos that enabled the bombers to venture out and destroy the enemy in their jungle bases.

The 9th PRS took its Lightnings to war over India – another rugged, and basically forgotten, combat zone where, once again, there was no quarter, and a downed pilot usually remained permanently missing. Flying high above oft-uncharted territory, American pilots ventured out and headed

Seen on a test flight from Burbank, this F-5A-10-LO shows just how much the Haze Paint darkened when flying at higher altitudes – the change of light had a great effect on these colours. Also of note are the camera ports and the way the white stencil instructions stand out against the blue paint

RIGHT This interesting aircraft modification was apparently undertaken in the field to enable the pilot of a standard P-38 to record the results of strafing and low-level bombing attacks. One of the nose-mounted .50 cals was removed, and replaced by a movie camera under a handmade blister – the aluminium strip covering the blister aperture was removed prior to flight to give a relatively clear field of view. This photo was taken on 14 May 1945

LEFT The Lockheed pilot of this factory-fresh F-5B brought his mount in close to the Lockheed PV-1 camera-ship so that Erik Miller could obtain this classic portrait. Note the heavy exhaust staining already starting to build up immediately aft of the turbosuperchargers

RIGHT This dramatic aerial view of the first F-5G illustrates the ports for the cameras under the greatly extended nose. The ADF loop can also be seen to the rear of the fuselage pod in front of the three recognition lights

towards pockets of enemy strength, where they attempted to penetrate defences and precisely fly their aircraft so that the resulting photos would be of usable quality to analyse.

Operating out of Britain, the Ninth Air Force flew four squadrons of photo Lightnings ,and the 30th, 31st, 33rd and 34th PRSs operated on a daily basis over 'Fortress Europe', bringing back intelligence essential for bombing missions, as well as vital information for formulating the coming invasion. After D-Day, these units moved directly into France, where they often operated from improvised airstrips in order to supply the Allied command with the latest reconnaissance.

America supplied some of its Allies with photo Lightnings, and the Royal Australian Air Force operated a few for a brief period of time in the Pacific. However, it was the Free French Air Force that achieved the best success with their 'photo birds', operating far and wide over Nazi territory, and returning with vital information needed to defeat the hated enemy. French F-5s flew alongside the Lightnings of the 3rd PRG, Twelfth Air Force, and the unit's distinguished commander, and famed novelist, Commandant Antoine de Saint-Exupery, simply disappeared during one such Lightning mission.

The photo Lightnings greatly contributed to the final Allied victory against both the Germans and the Japanese but, after the conclusion of the conflict, the prop-driven photo-recon fleet was of little importance, and the majority of these heroic veterans were simply blown up at their bases, rather than returned to the United States to be scrapped.

Despite this ignominious end, the photo Lightning had taught Lockheed the importance of aerial recon, and its postwar designs, overseen by 'Kelly' Johnson, would dominate the field.

HAZE CAMOUFLAGE

Since the photo fighters were going to venture into enemy territory unarmed, a great deal of thought was given to trying to make them 'invisible' through the application of special paints that would 'blend' the aircraft into the sky. The new camouflage was known as Haze Paint. The original application of Haze Paint was a rather complex affair, with the aircraft having to be painted overall black, with a thin coat of Haze then being applied over the top and down the sides of the airframe, which resulted in the finish being a very dark blue colour. Heavy Haze was then sprayed on the under surfaces and the remainder of the Lightning, producing a very light blue colour. The point between the heavy and light coats of haze was then sprayed with a medium coat of the paint, and the resulting colour was a medium blue shade.

Needless to say this process was time consuming, for it took a full working day just to let the paint dry. Extreme quality control and good lighting was also necessary to allow the paint to be applied according to specifications. The finish

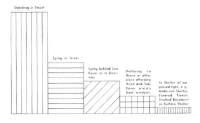
itself quickly changed colour and weathered badly in the sun.

A nasty surprise also awaited the originators of the camouflage, for testing soon proved that at over 20,000 ft, the Lightning actually became *more* visible, for the paint was much more intense in colour due to changes in lighting!

During October 1942, Lockheed was told to drop the Haze Paint and replace the colour scheme with ordinary Olive Drab and Neutral Grey camouflage. However, the military was still not convinced that Haze Paint was all that bad – anything that gave the unarmed photo Lightnings an extra chance was seriously considered.

Sherman-Williams Paint Company and the AAF came up with 'Synthetic Haze Paint', this colour scheme consisting of a Sky Base Blue and a synthetic Haze enamel called Flight Blue. The Lightning test aircraft was painted overall Sky Base Blue, and then Flight Blue was sprayed over the shadow areas of the aircraft and light coats were applied to the sides of the fuselage pod and booms. The new combination seemed to work fairly well, and it was adopted in March 1943 as the official paint scheme for the F-5.

However, the interpretation of this scheme was open to question and, depending on if the aircraft was painted at the factory or in the field or modification depot, there was a wide difference of application style. As the war progressed, Synthetic Haze Paint was dropped, and the photo Lightnings were instead delivered in natural metal finish.

LEFT AND ABOVE Camouflaging the vast Lockheed plant and conducting effective air raid drills became a part of life at Burbank, particularly in the early years of the war

CHAPTER ⬚11⬚ ACE OF ACES

RICHARD IRA BONG WAS born on 24 September 1920 on a farm near the rural community of Poplar, Wisconsin. As a young man, Bong graduated from Superior Central High School during 1938 and entered State Teachers' College with the hope of obtaining a teaching credential. However, with the increasing military build-up sweeping the nation, Bong enlisted in the Army Reserve at Wausau, Wisconsin, on 29 May 1941. At some stage, Bong had become extremely interested in aircraft, and duly requested pilot training. Accordingly, he was sent to Tulare, California, where he completed his primary pilot training on 16 August 1941.

Shipping next to Gardner Field, California, Bong started receiving basic training on 19 August, and this continued until 31 October 1941, at which time he headed for Luke Field, in Arizona, for advanced training (Class 42-A) – the course lasted from 4 November 1941 to 9 January 1942. On the latter date he was commissioned a second lieutenant in the Air Corps Reserve and rated as a pilot.

After receiving his commission, he was immediately called to extended active duty and given an assignment as a flying instructor at Luke Field. On 2 May 1942, the Bong transferred to Hamilton Field, near San Francisco, for combat training in the new Lockheed P-38. This course lasted four months, and after successfully completing the training in early September, he was alerted for foreign service and departed the United States for duty in the Pacific.

Upon arriving at Brisbane, in Australia, Bong was assigned to the 9th FS of the 49th FG as a combat fighter pilot. However, on 14 November 1942 he was reassigned to the 39th FS/35th FG at Port Moresby, in New Guinea, and it was with this unit that he scored his first victories. On 27 December Bong encountered and destroyed a Japanese 'Val' and 'Zeke' near Dobodura, on the north-eastern coast of New Guinea, while flying P-38F–5-LO s/n 42-12624 – he would destroy five Japanese aircraft before going back to the 9th FS on 11 January 1943. Bong continued to fly with the 9th, and its P-38s, until 11 November 1943, when he was given 60 days leave and reassigned to Headquarters, Fifth

ABOVE Classic combat photograph of Richard Bong (standing on the wing with hands on hips) after the pilot had returned from a fighter sweep on 12 April 1944 during which he had destroyed a Japanese 'Oscar' and damaged two others over Tanamerah Bay, New Guinea. Aircraft is P-38J-15-LO USAAF s/n 42-104380 – one of several such Lightnings flown by the ace. Spinners, wing tips, fin and rudder tips were all painted red

LEFT Following the mission of 11 March 1943, 'Dick' Bong poses for a photograph while reading a booklet. These four 9th FS pilots had just accounted for five Japanese aircraft during a raid on Dobodura airstrip. They are, from left to right; Lt T R Fowler (1), Capt Sidney Woods (1), Lt J C Mankin (1) and Lt Bong (2). Both Woods and Mankin would also finish the war as aces

ABOVE On 6 March 1943 Bong took time out to pose in full flight gear in the cockpit of a P-38G. Note the restraining cord on the canopy hatch

LEFT Gen Paul Wurtsmith, Fifth Air Force Fighter Commander, awards Bong the Distinguished Service Cross for his mission of 26 July 1943 when he destroyed two 'Tonys' and two Zeros. Bong would go home on leave soon after this photo was taken, having downed 21 Japanese aircraft in just over 11 months of combat

RIGHT Bong's most famous Lightning was P-38J-15-LO USAAF s/n 42-103993, which he named *Marge* after his fiancee Marge Vattendahl. The 25 victory flags date the photograph as having been taken after 3 April 1944

BELOW In June 1944 Bong visited the Lockheed factory at Burbank to extol the virtues of the P-38 to the workers that built the aircraft

During his brief time at Lockheed, Bong gave his now-wife Marge a ride in a Lightning. Sitting on the shelf behind the pilot was not the most comfortable of positions, and note the piece of foam stuck to the canopy hatch to protect the passenger's head

Fighter Command in New Guinea as Assistant A-3 in charge of replacement aircraft. While holding this assignment, Bong kept flying combat missions, and increased his victory score to 28 confirmed aircraft. This was major news back home, since Bong had at last broken famed World War 1 ace Eddie Rickenbacker's record of 26 (German) aircraft destroyed.

In April 1944 Bong returned to the United States and was assigned to the Matagorda Peninsula Bombing Range, Foster Field, Texas, for the purpose of receiving and checking on the latest gunnery methods and instructions. In September 1944, Bong, now promoted to major, returned to his assignment with Fifth Fighter Command in the Pacific, and was placed in charge of gunnery training with that organisation. In addition to his duties as gunnery instructor – and although not required, or expected, to perform combat duty – he voluntarily flew 30 more combat missions over Borneo and the Philippine Islands, destroying a dozen more enemy aircraft and bringing his final total to 40 destroyed – his last victory was over a Ki-43 'Oscar' on 17 December 1944.

For his achievements during this third tour of overseas duty, Major Bong was awarded the Medal of Honor, which was presented to him by Gen Douglas MacArthur. After completing over 200 combat missions for a total of over 500 combat hours (with 734 hours, 35 minutes, first pilot time), he was released from his assignment with Fifth Fighter Command in December

1944 and returned to the United States for an extensive series of War Bond tours.

Once back in the USA, Maj Bong was assigned to the 4020th Army Air Force Base Unit at Wright Field, Ohio, as a test pilot, where he made functional tests and undertook ferry missions with single- and twin-engined fighters. On 23 June 1945 Bong was transferred to Burbank, California, and given an assignment as Chief of Flight Operations, Office of the Army Air Force Plant Representative, at Lockheed. Since the company was engaged in the development and manufacture of the new P-80 Shooting Star jet fighter, Bong received a full training course prescribed for the new aircraft at Muroc AAF Base in the Mojave Desert.

Back at Burbank, Bong began to settle into the testing of the new jet. However, there were numerous problems, and the AAF was worried about the programme since, by 2 August, seven P-80s had been destroyed, an equal number had been damaged and five pilots had been killed. On 6 August Bong strapped into a P-80A-1-LO for a routine test flight. Col Charles Langmack recalled;

'When Maj Bong came to Lockheed, he was assigned to my office – the Army Air Force Plant Representative's Office. I assigned him to Flight Operations to fly acceptance flights on P-38 and P-80 aircraft.

'I was in charge of all flying of AAF aircraft built by Lockheed, and was also president of the AAF accident investigation board which investigated the subject P-80 crash.

'Richard Bong and I were in flight operations at the same time. He was clearing for his P-80 acceptance flight and I was filing a flight plan to one of Lockheed's sub plants with a C-47 staff ship.

'My C-47 was parked near the intersection of the east-west/north-south runways. I was still looking over or checking a few things on my airplane when Bong went by on the take-off run. I watched as he cleared the boundary okay and then, just a second or two later, the engine quit just as he had started a very shallow right turn at 50 to 60 ft altitude, and no where near efficient climbing speed.

'Within a split second after the engine quit, the P-80 stalled and went in at a very steep angle, striking the ground with terrific impact and fuel explosion. Richard's body was well within the radius of scattered parts of the airplane, which covered approximately a block-and-a-half in diameter. Obviously there was no time to bail out of the plane.

'The airplane's powerplant was a General Electric Type I-40. The AAF investigation did not find conclusive information that Richard Bong failed to turn on the boost pump for backup on take-off.'

The death of America's top ace was eclipsed in the news since 6 August 1945 was also the date that the first atomic bomb was dropped on Hiroshima.

ABOVE Milo Burcham and Bong check out the new dive flaps being installed at the factory on all P-38J-25-LOs and P-38Ls. At this time kits were being sent into the field to allow the flaps to be installed on earlier P-38Js

CHAPTER 12

RIDERS OF THE STORM

Classic photograph of a pre-war (US entry) Lockheed P-38 Air Corps pilot fastening his parachute harness. The early model Lightning was camouflaged in Olive Drab and Neutral Grey, and carries two stripes on the booms – probably denoting that the aircraft was the mount of a squadron commander. The fastidious flight coveralls seen in this photograph would be a far cry from the eclectic garb worn by war-time Lightning pilots. Note the flight chart stuck in the pilot's left leg pocket

ABOVE Pre-war Lightning pilots receive instructions from a Lt Giusti prior to taking off for practice manoeuvres. The pilots (again note the relative uniformity of their garb) all have squadron patches on the right chest pockets of their leather A-2 jackets, but these are unfortunately obscured by Mae West life preservers – the insignia on the camouflaged P-38's coolant radiator shroud is also effectively blotted out by a 'strategically placed' pilot

LEFT Loading .50 cal ammunition into a magazine in the Lightning's nose. Although camouflaged in the flat Olive Drab and Neutral Grey scheme which soon weath-ered and chipped, this pre-war Lightning is in relatively pristine condition. Note that the inside of the gun bay access panel was sprayed with zinc chromate

LEFT With its fuselage pod and two engine nacelles, the Lightning made a great 'canvas' for squadron artists. P-38L-5-LO USAAF s/n 44-25638 *ALMOST 'A' DRAGGIN/"KITTIE"* was flown by Maj C M Isaacson, who had scored four victories when he posed with his aircraft. Clayton Isaacson flew 50 B-25 missions with the 321st BG in North Africa before volunteering for a second tour. He was sent to Italy, where he was put in command of the 96th FS/82nd FG. While flying with that unit, he became an ace on 20 July 1944 when he downed a Bf 109 for his fifth victory. Upon returning to the States, he volunteered for another tour and was sent to the Philippines in February 1945 to assume command of the 7th FS/49th FG, with whom he flew a further 80 missions. Isaacson finished the war with five confirmed and one and one shared damaged. He returned to combat during the Korean War, flying an additional 75 missions with the 51st FG. As chief tactical inspector for the Fifth Air Force, Isaacson also completed a further 50 missions in seven United Nations types – Mustang, Shooting Star, Thunderjet, Sabre, USMC Corsair and Panther, and RAAF Gloster Meteor. During 1964, he was commander of the joint American-Belgium Paratroop Task Force, and led the rescue of 1800 hostages held by terrorists in the Congo. Truly a man of action, Clayton 'Ike' Isaacson retired from the USAF in July 1970 with the rank of brigadier general

OPPOSITE BELOW The unsung groundcrews had to keep their Lightnings in the best condition possible, no matter what the environment. During the deadly European winter of 1944/45, the crew of this 429th FS/474th FG Lightning struggle against the Belgian weather to service and rearm 'their' fighter prior to its next mission

BELOW Laurence Elroy 'Scrappy' Blumer was sent to England in March 1944 to join the 367th FG's 393rd FS. On 23 August 1944 he destroyed an amazing five Focke-Wulf Fw 190s in just ten minutes near St Quentin. Soon after this action, he was promoted to captain and then to

major in December. A 'colourful character' who had trained on P-39s with Chuck Yeager at Tonapah, in Nevada, Blumer went through five P-38s during his tour of duty. He assumed command of the squadron during November 1944, and scored one further victory over an Fw 190 on 19 November. A nattily attired Blumer is seen with his highly-decorated *SCRAPIRON IV* at Juvincourt, in France, in late 1944. In 1969 Blumer acquired ex-Honduran Air Force P-38L USAAF s/n 44-26961 and had the aircraft finished in these markings. He flew the fighter for several years, before selling it on in the early 1970s – it was subsequently written off in April 1981

LEFT Seen in full flight gear, Maj R C Rogers poses with his P-38J, which was named *"LITTLE BUCKAROO"*, and carried elaborate nose art, along with bomb and victory mission symbols. This view shows the fillet between the wing centre section and fuselage pod that was added to eliminate tail buffet. The fillet had to be carefully hand-fitted, and carried large 'no step' stencils

LEFT CENTRE P-38J-15-LO USAAF s/n 43-104308, nicknamed 'Gentle Annie', was the mount of Col Harold J Rau, commanding officer of the 20th FG. Rau is seen here with his groundcrew, TSgt James A Douglas, Sgt Grant L Beach and SSgt Luther W Ghent, and his dog, at Kingscliffe during April 1944. The camouflaged aircraft is fitted with external tanks and has had the nose cone polished in the hope that *Luftwaffe* pilots would think the aircraft was an unarmed photo-recon Lightning

BELOW Lt Noble, his crew and the very decorated *Miss Mass*, which also bears various other names. Typical of other United Kingdom-based Lightnings, USAAF s/n 42-67449 shows the effects of hard weather and hard missions. Note the P-38 engine cowlings scattered in the background

RIGHT They had what it took. Pilots celebrate the downing of another Nazi aircraft, while a well-used P-38F stands guard in the background. *Shoot .. YOU'RE FADED* was flown by Lt John A MacKay, who scored five kills while flying P-38s with the 27th FS/1st FG, Twelfth Air Force

LEFT A pleased Lt W G Broome and his P-38G following a successful ground attack mission. Nose art consists of two martini glasses, being tipped in a toast, with the inscription *TO THE QUEEN ANN* between them

ABOVE An imaculately uniformed Capt Newell Roberts settles into the seat of a factory-fresh Lightning at the Burbank plant. On a war bond tour, Roberts was one of the first aces of the North African campaign, destroying five aircraft, claiming a sixth as a probable and damaging a seventh by 15 February 1943. After the war, Roberts became a medical doctor. This view shows the factory stencilling to advantage, along with the dust shroud over the instrument panel

RIGHT Striking an aggressive stance, Maj Herbert E Johnson is seen with his Lightning after a mission to Brunswick, Germany, that had seen him destroy two Fw 190s

ABOVE Among the more bizarre incidents of the Pacific War was when famed aviator Charles Lindbergh destroyed a Japanese aircraft in combat. Lindbergh, who had fallen into disfavour before America's entry into the war due his pro-German, pro-peace statements, was in the Pacific in a purely civilian capacity to instruct Lightning and Corsair pilots on how to increase their aircraft's range and engine life by using correct throttle settings (he was able to show them how to increase their range by up to 50 per cent). During a flight with other Lightnings, Lindbergh encountered a Japanese fighter and destroyed it. Since he was a civilian, this was in direct conravention of the Geneva Convention, but since the Japanese had not signed the latter agreement, it probably did not make any difference. The air force was, however, anxious to make sure that the event did not receive publicity, and the victory was not added to the USAAF's final wartime tally! The long-distance flyer is seen here with Thomas McGuire who, with 38 victories, was America's second-ranking ace behind Dick Bong. During the 'ace race' with the latter pilot, Maj McGuire made a determined effort to raise his score as high as possible whilst Bong was back in the United States. However on 7 January 1945, McGuire committed a basic error that ended the race. He and three other Lightning pilots were dogfighting with a single Japanese Ki-43 over Los Negros Island, in the Philippines, when he racked his P-38 into too tight a turn, entered a high-speed stall, and flat spun into the jungle below

ABOVE RIGHT Lt Don Warner with his *Cutie Connie* 'somewhere in the Pacific'. The aircraft carries three victory markings over Japanese aircraft, along with the silhouette of a Japanese destroyer, which the pilot had sunk – the Lightning's concentrated firepower did a great deal of damage to enemy shipping

LEFT Crew chief TSgt Hank Jolly and P-38L-5-LO USAAF s/n 44-25470 *PUTT PUTT MARU*, which was the mount of Charles Henry 'Mac' MacDonald. Col MacDonald was commanding officer of the 475th FG at the time this photo was taken, and the aircraft is seen carrying 26 victory symbols. The colonel was sent on forced leave to the United States from August to October 1944 as punishment for allowing Charles Lindbergh to fly a combat mission, and shoot down a Japanese aircraft

RIGHT Photographed during June 1942 at an Australian base, photo-recon pilot Capt Karl Polifka relaxes after outrunning two flights of Japanese Zeros over Rabaul with his damaged Lightning. Polifka would become one of the USAAF's most experienced photo-recon pilots by war's end

BELOW RIGHT Doesn't look like fun! Famed *Life* magazine photographed 1st Lt David Douglas Duncan of the USMC wanted to take some dramatic photos of Marine Corsairs launching rockets against Japanese targets. Accordingly, a drop tank was extensively modified to make room for Duncan and his camera. However, he had no communication with the pilot. During the mission, the latter positioned the Lightning behind the Corsair, which was in a slight dive, and when the F4U fired its salvo of rockets, the turbulence nearly flipped the P-38L on its back! Fortunately, the pilot recovered, and Duncan had gotten his dramatic photo

LEFT Taking a break from changing spark plugs on the Lightning's two Allisons, TSgt D C Todd is seen with the Lightning flown by Maj G Laren Jr. Note the five Japanese victory markings, along with an impressive tally of enemy locomotives. Since Maj Laren's name does not appear on the USAF's official ace lists, these victories were probably claimed during ground attacks – a hazardous enough undertaking, given the P-38's vulnerable liquid-cooling tubing and radiators

CHAPTER 13 FRONTLINE

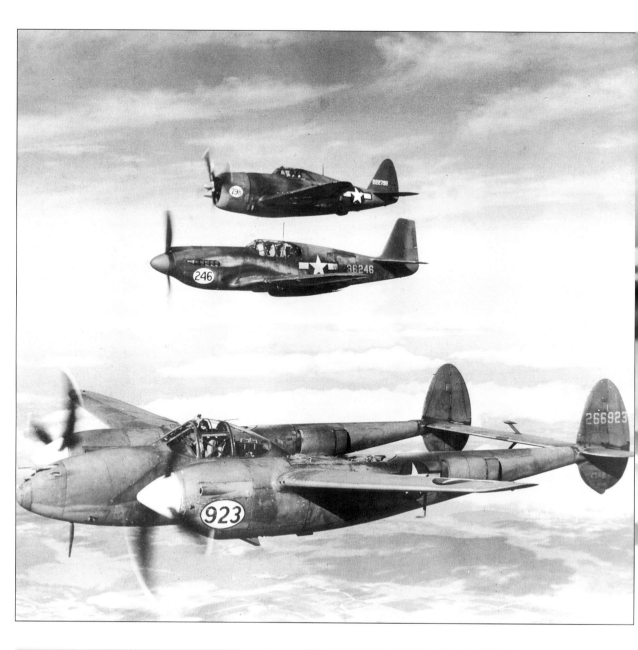

LEFT Training new Lightning pilots posed something of a problem for the Air Corps, as they had no suitable twin-engine trainer when the P-38 started entering service. There was certainly nothing in the inventory that could match the aircraft's performance, or handling characteristics. As a result, early training was rather basic. The prospective P-38 pilot was required to spend a minimum of five hours in a P-38 cockpit, becoming acquainted with instruments and cockpit installations. This, according to instructors, would make him feel at home on his first solo flight so as to be able to respond correctly to emergencies. The instructor emphasised the necessity for developing a thorough cockpit routine, and 'beat it into the head' of the trainee to always check the cockpit from left to right while utilising the checklist. The next step for the trainee was to pass a blindfold test, and then it was on to a 'piggy-back' flight, where the trainee was taught to know what the instructor was doing from the time of entering the cockpit until the flight was over. The trainee had to wear a B-8 pack back parachute and, if a problem was encountered, was instructed to bail out before the pilot. However, if the trainee was too large the pilot would go first, while the trainee would reach forward and steady the control wheel! After the 'piggy-back' flight, the trainee moved on to his first P-38 flight. This photograph shows early versions of the Lightning (P-38H-5-LO), Mustang, and Thunderbolt being used in the training role at Orlando, Florida – the site of the USAAF's Tactical Training Center, where pilots were given instruction in the fighter-bomber role

ABOVE Sergeant pilots relax on the desert floor of Muroc Army Air Force Base (now Edwards AFB) as they watch four P-38Fs from the 95th FS return after a training mission on 12 March 1943

OPPOSITE TOP One can almost feel the immediate postwar tension in the air in William T Larkins' photograph of a freshly-camouflaged P-38D seen at the Oakland Naval Air Station, California, on 16 November 1941. The aircraft had been carrying the pre-war identifier 99-51P on the vertical fins, but this had been quickly sanded off in favour of security. The identifier meant that the aircraft was assigned to the 16th Pursuit Squadron/51st Pursuit Group out of March Field. This P-38D was a long way from being operational, since the guns had not yet been installed – aerodynamic tubes had taken their place

OPPOSITE CENTRE P-38F USAAC s/n 41-7498, assigned to the 94th FS, is seen in Sardinia during 1943 with its pilot, Lt J Hagenback. Note the later Type 4 national insignia, which was introduced on 17 September 1943. The 94th operated Lightnings from 1941 through to 1945. Even though the aircraft were being flown in extremely harsh conditions, the groundcrew has kept it fairly clean. Many 94th Lightnings were highly decorated with individual markings, and *BAT OUT OF HELL* is no exception to this rule

OPPOSITE BELOW Operating from rough and unimproved fields caused some trouble, as illustrated by P-38H-5-LO USAAF s/n 42-67034, which had its nose gear collapse at Mateur airfield in North Africa during 1943. The aircraft was assigned to the 1st FG at the time, as indicated by

the boom bands and painted wing tips. The irregular patch in front of the windshield was a poison gas detector

ABOVE Lightnings were tested and cleared for extreme cold weather operations, and early variants of the fighter were flown to bases in Alaska for operations against invading Japanese in the very hostile environment of the Aleutians

ABOVE The 39th FS was the first unit to operate the Lightning in the South West Pacific, receiving 25 P-38s in August 1942. The unit quickly took the war to the Japanese over the skies of eastern New Guinea once equipped with the new fighter. This 39th often decorated its aircraft with fearsome 'sharksmouths' on the engine cowlings, and utilised individual aircraft numbers between 10 and 39

OPPOSITE TOP During the early stages of the war, the USAAF tested many of its fighter aircraft with ski installations to see if the aircraft could operate in cold and snowy environments. For the most part, the tests proved that such operations were feasible, but not overly practical. As part of these trials, P-38J-1-LO is seen filled with skis – note the hydraulic rams that raised and lowered the skis to fit against the booms and nose

RIGHT Due to its large surface areas, the Lightning became one of the most decorated of all wartime American combat aircraft. This P-38L was assigned to the 36th FS/8th FG at Ie Shima when it was photographed during 1945. The salt-laden atmosphere of the Pacific quickly caused surface corrosion of the unprotected natural aluminium skin, but the military adopted the view that these aircraft were very expendable and short-lived, so little effort was made to protect them for long-term operations

BELOW As with any other American World War 2 military aircraft, the P-38 suffered its fair share of accidents. Here, a Ninth Air Force Lightning has crashed into gasoline trucks at its Belgium base while trying to land in poor weather upon returning from a ground attack mission during December 1944

BOTTOM Happy to be alive. Lt James Posten waves from the cockpit of his P-38J-15-LO that he has just belly-landed next to a beach after the aircraft suffered battle damage during a Pacific patrol. Unable to make it back to his home airfield, Posten put the fighter down in a text-book example of a perfect crash

landing. The aircraft carries the colourful pre-war style tail stripes utilised by the 9th FS/49th FG

RIGHT Col Harold Rau leads the 20th FG on a bombing mission during June 1944. Rau was flying a 'Droop Snoot' modified Lightning, with bombardier Capt Herschel Ezell in the nose, on this occasion. On the bombardier's signal, all the Lightnings in the formation would release their underwing bombs, resulting in a devastating strike on an enemy target

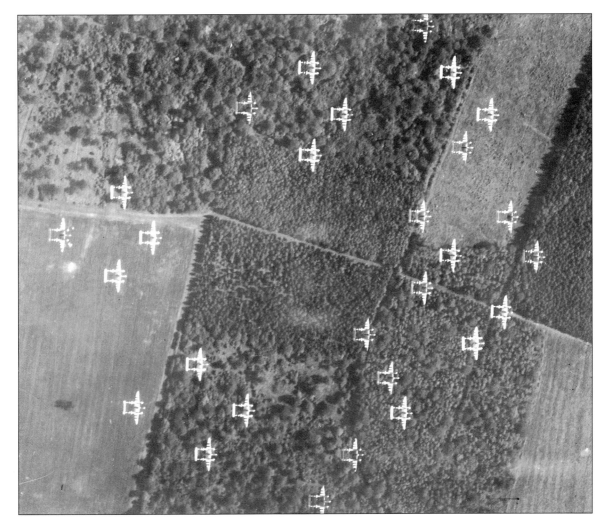

LEFT 'Droop Snoot' modifications were initially done 'in the field', and this resulted in several variations on the theme. This P-38J was the prototype conversion, and it is seen here at Langford Lodge, where it was being displayed to the USAAF. Fitted with a Norden bombsight, the bombardier's position was fairly accommodating, and a formation of P-38s (carrying one 2000-lb bomb and one drop tank) could unleash a very effective carpet bombing pattern when releasing on the lead aircraft. Because the P-38 carried just one pilot compared to the ten crew members on Liberators and 'Forts', the potential loss of life on such a mission was greatly reduced

BELOW Well-worn Olive Drab and Neutral Gray P-38Js of the 383rd FS/364th FG head out from Britain on a mission. 'N2' was the squadron coding while 'K' was the individual aircraft letter, repeated on the insides of the vertical fins. The squadron's identifying geometric symbol was a large white circle painted on the verticals, which unfortunately obscured the serial number. The factory construction number is,

however, still carried on the nose of the P-38 closest to the camera

BOTTOM Shortly after the end of the war in Europe, P-38L-5-LO USAAF s/n 44-25545 was photographed prowling over German territory

ABOVE This magnificent view of F-5Bs in formation over France was taken in October 1944. The lead aircraft is F-5B-15-LO

USAAF s/n 44-28624, and all three Lightnings were assigned to the 34th PRS/10th PRG, based at Dijon. The 34th flew the F-5 from 1943 through to 1945, and had started life as the 126th Observation Squadron, Wisconsin National Guard, on 30 June 1940 – it had been redesignated the 34th PRS on 11 August 1943. The unit reverted back to being the 126th FS, Wisconsin Air National Guard on 24 May 1946.

Photographed from a Texan, the Lightnings have their flaps down, and it is interesting to note the different angles of attack adopted by the pilots to remain in formation with the much slower T-6

RIGHT Displaying its D-Day stripes to advantage, F-5E-1-LO *Flo Lou Marie* was assigned to the 7th PRG, based at Mount Farm airfield, just south of Oxford, in England. The aircraft was photographed from another F-5 during October 1944 whilst flying near to its base

ABOVE Natural-metal F-6L-1-LO USAAF s/n 44-24274 was photographed in clear skies over Germany soon after VE-Day. It was ssigned to the 31st PRS/67th TRG, the unit having flown the P-38/F-4/F-5/F-6 from 1943 through to 1945

BELOW Finished in an overall light blue scheme applied in the field, F-5E-2-LO USAAF s/n 43-28333 *Lanakila* operated from Mount Farm with the 7th PRG throughout much of 1944. Note the covers over the camera port glass and the

detailed mission marker board immediately below the cockpit

ABOVE End of the line #1. With the war against Germany over, the majority of photo-recon Lightnings were stripped of useful equipment and then rendered unusable through the simple expedient of lobbing a live grenade into the cockpit. This 33rd PRS Lightning has had its cameras removed and its Allisons chopped off – hence its nose-high attitude. The USAAF judged that the F-5 was obsolete, and therefore simply not worth taking back to the USA for scrapping

RIGHT End of the line #2. Virtually new P-38Js are seen after then had been pushed off a cliff at Clark Field, in the Philippines. The aircraft were then set on fire, before being bulldozed into the ground

APPENDICES

LIGHTNING VARIANTS

XP-38

Highly advanced long-range fighter with two Allison V12 engines (propellers rotating toward fuselage pod), with provision for two .50 cal/two .30 cal and one 23 mm weapon (never installed). Quickly set records but was destroyed on 11 February 1939. Highly-polished natural metal finish. Model 022-64-01.

YP-38-LO

Thirteen pre-production service test aircraft (Model 122-62-02). Delivered in polished natural aluminum finish, with standard Air Corps markings. Allison engines equipped with outward rotating propellers/B-2 turbosuperchargers. Armament as per prototype, but with replacement of 23 mm cannon with 37 mm unit.

P-38-LO

First production version (Model 222-62-02) with 30 built. Very limited armour protect/four .50 cal and one 37 mm weapons. Delivered in Olive Drab and Neutral Grey camouflage. Most used for training and testing.

XP-38A-LO

Experimental modification of P-38-LO 40-762 to test pressurised cockpit (622-62-10).

P-38D-LO

Model 222-62-08. Basically the same as P-38-LO, but with more military equipment added, including self-sealing tanks/extra armour. Flares were also added, along with a low-pressure oxygen system.

P-38E-LO

Basically the same as the P-38D, but hydraulic system reworked. 37 mm cannon replaced with 20 mm cannon.

Most fitted with SCR274N radio. 210 built, and some converted as F-4-1-LO.

P-38F-LO

Model 222-60-09. Variants of the F received new model numbers. F-1 became 222-60-15 and F-5 222-60-12, whilst other models became 322-16-19. Pylons inboard of the engines for the carriage of up to 2000-lb bombs or drop tanks. F-15 saw introduction of modified Fowler flaps.

P-38G-LO

Basically the same as F, except for new engines (V-1710-51/55) and revised internal radio gear. G received Model number 222-68-12 (G-12 and G-15 were 322-68-19, these being undelivered Lightning Mk IIs).

P-38H-LO

Model 422-81-20. Powered by two V-1710-89/91 engines with automatic oil radiator gills for improved cooling. Underwing provisions increased to load of 3200 lbs. 601 built, and 128 finished, or converted, as F-5C-LOs.

P-38J-LO

Model 422-81-14 covered J-1 and J-5, 422-81-22 the J-10, 522-81-22 the J-15 and -20, and 522-87-23 the J-25. The J introduced the most distinctive physical change in the Lightning – the large chin radiators for improved cooling. All J variants, except J-1, had more fuel capacity. With the J-10, a flat optically-perfect bullet-proof windscreen panel was introduced. J-25 had new dive flaps and power-assisted ailerons. Majority delivered in natural metal finish. Total of 2970 built, including F-5E/F-5F variants.

P-38K-LO

One only, Model 422-85-22. Basically the same as P-38J, but with V-1710-75/77 engines equipped with paddle-blade propellers. Earlier XP-38K-LO was a P-38E conversion.

P-38L-LO/VN

Model 422-87-23. Basically the same as P-38J, but with V-1710-111/113 engines. Landing light now in port wing. 3810 L-LOs were built and 113 L-VNs were constructed by Vultee. Connections for ten 5-inch underwing rockets.

P-38M-LO

Model 522-87-23 was a conversion of the P-38L into a two-seat nightfighter (approximately 75 built), with radar mounted under nose in pod. Majority had solid black finish.

OTHER VARIANTS

XFO-1

Five F-5B-LOs assigned to the US Navy in North Africa with Bureau Numbers 01209 through to 01212.

F-4-1-LO

Unarmed photo variant of P-38E, fitted with four K-17 cameras and autopilot. F-4-1-LO/Model 222-62-13/ numbered 99 aircraft, with serials 41-2098 and 2099, 2121 to 2156, 2158 to 2171, 2173 to 2218 and 2220. F-4A-1-LO used the P-38F as the basic airframe, and 20 were built (41-2362 to 2381). Most delivered in Haze camouflage.

F-5A

Modified from P-38G with 20 F-5A-1-LOs (s/n 42-12667 to 12686) and 140 F-5A-10-LOs (s/n 42-12967 to 12986, 42-13067 to 13126, and 42-13267 to 13326) as Model 222-68-16. Single F-5A-2-LO (Model 222-62-16) was modified from P-38E s/n 41-2157. Most delivered in Haze camouflage.

F-5B

P-38J-10-LO modified for photo-recon. Designated Model 422-81-21, and 200 built (s/n 42-76312 to 67401, and 42-68192 to 68301).

F-5C

Model 222-68-16, photo-recon based on P-38H, with 123 built.

XF-5D

Model 222-68-16. Rebuild of the F-5A-10-LO, with plexiglass nose cone and prone observer's position. Two .50 cal guns and a vertical camera fitted.

F-5E

Photo-recon modification of the P-38J. F-5E-2-LO was Model 422-81-22 (P-38J-15-LO), with 100 built. F-5E-3-LO

Model 522-87-23 was a conversion of 105 J-25-LO airframes. F-5E-4-LO Model 422-87-23 was a conversion of 500 P-38L-1-LOs.

F-5F-3-LO

Model 422-87-23 photo-recon modification of the P-38L-5-LO.

F-5G-6-LO

Model 422-87-23. Basically the same as the F-5F-3-LO, but different cameras.

Model 322

Lightning for the RAF. 243 Mk Is were ordered (AE978 to 999, and AF100 to 220), but just three were delivered. The the rest were taken over by the USAAF as P-322 and flown in the training role. An order for 524 Mk IIs (AF221 to 744) was cancelled.

LIGHTNING SERIAL NUMBERS

XP-38-LO	37-457
YP-38-LO	39-689 to -701
P-38-LO	40-744 to -773
XP-38A-LO	40-762
P-38D-LO	40-774 to -809
P-38E-LO	41-1983 to -2097, 41-2100 to -2120, 41-2172, 41-2219, and 41-2221 to -2292
P-38F-LO	41-2293 to -2321
P-38F-1-LO	41-2322
P-38F-LO	41-2323 to -2358
P-38F-1-LO	41-2359 to -2361
P-38F-LO	41-2382 to -2386
P-38F-1-LO	41-2387
P-38F-LO	41-2388 to -2392
P-38F-1-LO	41-7484 to -7485
P-38F-LO	41-7486 to -7496
P-38F-1-LO	41-7497
P-38F-LO	41-7498 to -7513
P-38F-1-LO	41-7514 to -7515
P-38F-LO	41-7516 to -7524
P-38F-1-LO	41-7525
P-38F-1-LO	41-7536 to -7538
P-38F-1-LO	41-7539 to -7541
P-38F-LO	41-7542 to -7543
P-38F-1-LO	41-7544
P-38F-LO	41-7545 to -7547
P-38F-1-LO	41-7548 to -7550

P-38F-LO	41-7551
P-38F-1-LO	41-7552 to -7680
P-38F-5-LO	41-12567 to -12666
P-38F-13-LO	43-2035 to -2063
P-38F-15-LO	43-2064 to -2184
P-38G-1-LO	42-12687 to -12766
P-38G-3-LO	42-12787 to -12798
P-38G-5-LO	42-12799 to -12866
P-38G-10-LO	42-12870 to -12966,
	42-12987 to -13066,
	42-13127 to -13266
	and 42-13327 to -13557
P-38G-13-LO	43-2185 to -2358
P-38G-15-LO	43-2359 to -2558
P-38H-1-LO	42-13559, and 42-66502 to -66726
P-38H-5-LO	42-66727 to -67101
P-38J-1-LO	42-12867 to -12869, and
	42-13560 to -13566
P-38J-5-LO	42-67102 to -67311
P-38J-10-LO	42-67402 to -68191
P-38J-15-LO	42-103979 to -104428, 43-28248
	to -29047, and 44-23059 to -23208
P-38J-20-LO	44-23209 to -23558
P-38J-25-LO	44-23559 to -23768
YP-38K-LO	41-1983
P-38K-1-LO	42-13558
P-38L-1-LO	44-23769 to -25058
P-38L-5-LO	44-25059 to -27258, and
	44-53008 to -53327
P-38L-5-VN	43-50226 to -30338
P-38M-LO	44-25237 (converted from
	P-38L-5-LO - other serials random)

LIGHTNING SPECIFICATIONS

XP-38

Span	52 ft
Length	37 ft 10 in
Height	12 ft 10 in
Wing Area	327.5 sq ft
Empty Weight	11,507 lb
Loaded Weight	15,416 lb
Max Speed	413 mph
Ceiling	38,000 ft
Climb	20,000 ft in 6.5 min
Powerplants	Allison V-1710C-9 to -11/1150 hp

YP-38

Span	52 ft
Length	37 ft 10 in
Height	9 ft 10 in
Wing Area	327.5 sq ft
Empty Weight	11,171 lb
Loaded Weight	14,348 lb
Max Speed	405 mph
Cruise	330 mph
Ceiling	38,000 ft
Climb	3330 fpm (initial)
Range	650 miles
Powerplants	Allison V-1710-27 to -29/1150 hp

P-38

Overall Dimensions	as YP-38
Empty Weight	11,670 lb
Loaded Weight	15,340 lb
Max Speed	390 mph
Cruise	310 mph
Climb	3200 fpm (initial)
Range	825 to 1500 miles
Powerplants	Allison V-1710-27 to -29/1150 hp

P-38D

Overall Dimensions	as YP-38
Empty Weight	11,780 lb
Loaded Weight	15,500 lb
Max Speed	390 mph
Cruise	300 mph
Ceiling	39,000 ft
Climb	20,000 ft in 8 min
Range	400 to 975 miles
Powerplants	Allison V-1710-27 to -29/1150 hp

P-38E

Overall Dimensions	as YP-38
Empty Weight	11,880 lb
Loaded Weight	15,482 lb
Max Speed	395 mph
Range	500 miles
Powerplants	V-1710-27 to -29/1150 hp

P-38F

Overall Dimensions	as YP-38
Empty Weight	12,265 lb
Loaded Weight	18,000 lb
Max Speed	395 mph
Cruise	305 mph
Climb	20,000 ft in 8.8 min
Range	350 to 1900 miles
Powerplants	Allison V-1710-49 to -53/1325 hp

P-38G

Overall Dimensions	as YP-38
Empty Weight	12,200 lb
Loaded Weight	19,800 lb
Max Speed	400 mph
Cruise	340 mph
Climb	20,000 ft in 8.5 min
Range	275 to 2400 miles
Powerplants	Allison V-1710-51 to -55/1325 hp

P-38H

Overall Dimensions	as YP-38
Empty Weight	12,380 lb
Loaded Weight	120,300 lb
Max Speed	402 mph
Cruise	300 mph
Climb	2600 fpm (initial)
Range	300 to 2400 miles
Powerplants	Allison V-1710-89 to -91/1425 hp

P-38J

Overall Dimensions	as YP-38
Empty Weight	12,780 lb
Loaded Weight	21,600 lb
Max Speed	414 mph
Cruise	290 mph
Climb	20,000 ft in 7 min
Range	450 to 2600 miles
Powerplants	Allison V-1710-89 to -91/1425 hp

P-38L

Overall Dimensions	as YP-38
Empty Weight	12,800 lb
Loaded Weight	21,600 lb
Max Speed	414 mph
Climb	20,000 ft in 7 min
Range	450 to 2625 miles
Powerplants	Allison V-1710-111 to -173/1425 hp

EIGHTH, NINTH, TWELFTH AND FIFTEENTH AIR FORCE LIGHTNING UNIT CODES

38th FS/55th FG	CG
338th FS/55th FG	CL
343rd FS/55th FG	CY
551st FS/495th FG	DQ
48th FS/14th FG	ES
13th FS/7th FG	ES
27th FS/1st FG	HV
61st FS/56th FG	HV
55th FS/20th FG	KI
77th FS/20th FG	LC
71st FS/1st FG	LM
79th FS/20th FG	MC
49th FS/14th FG	QU
33rd PS/10th PG	SW
94th FS/1st FG	UN
34th PS/69th TRG	XX
554th FS/496th FTG	B9
402nd FS/370th FG	E6
429th FS/474th FG	F5
22nd PS/7th PG	G2
392nd FS/367th FG	H5
30th PS/10th PG	I6
435th FS/479th FG	J2
430th FS/474th FG	K6
434th FS/479th FG	L2
383rd FS/364th FG	N2
34th PS/10th PR	S9
33rd PS/363rd TRG	2W
394th FS/367th FG	4N
385th FS/364th FG	5E
384th FS/364th FG	5Y
485th FS/370th FG	7F
428th FS/474th FG	7Y
393rd FS/367th FG	8L
31st PS/67th TRG	8V
436th FS/479th FG	9B
401st FS/370th FG	9D

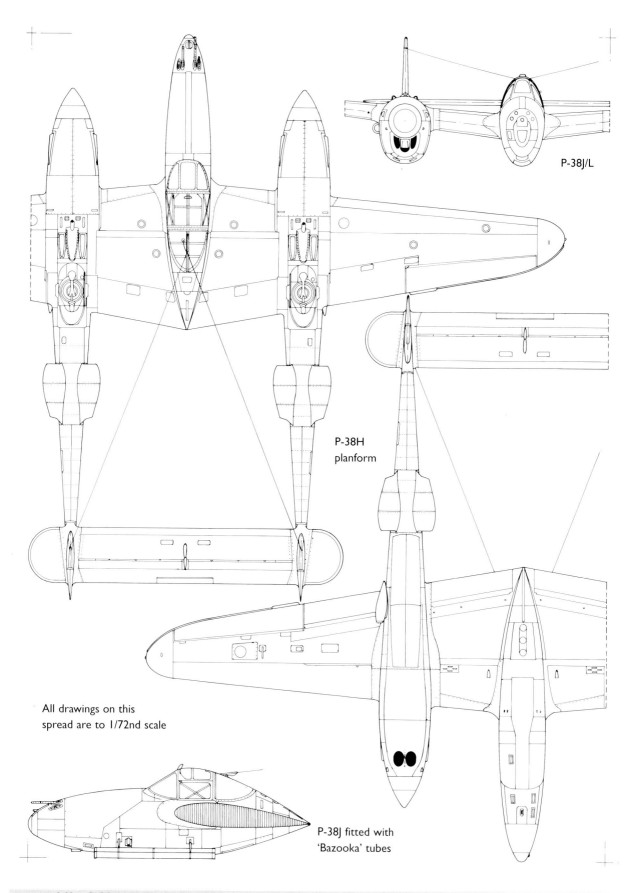

P-38J/L

P-38H
planform

All drawings on this
spread are to 1/72nd scale

P-38J fitted with
'Bazooka' tubes

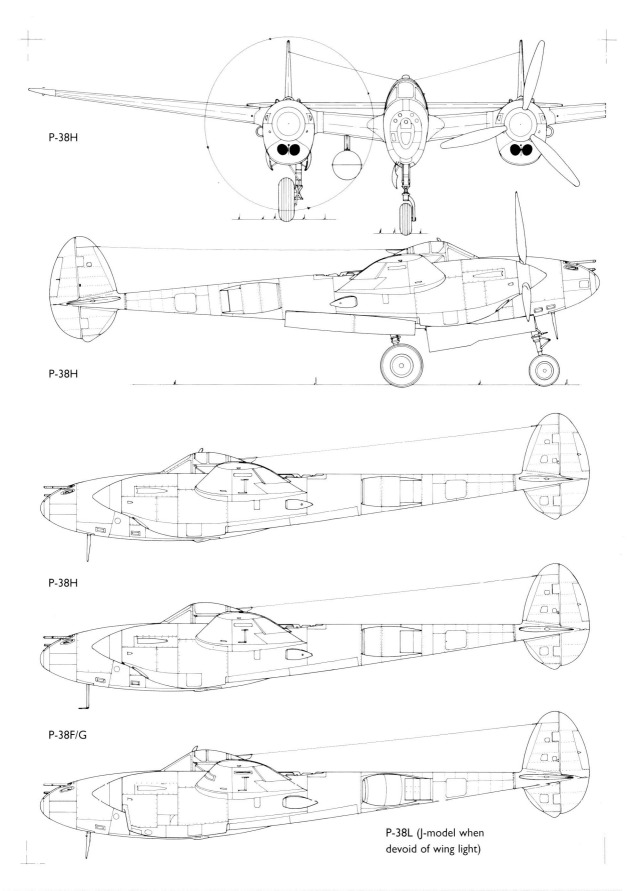

P-38H

P-38H

P-38H

P-38F/G

P-38L (J-model when
devoid of wing light)

Lockheed P-38J/L Lightning

Cutaway drawing by Mike Badrocke

1 Starboard navigation light
2 Starboard aileron
3 Aileron mass balance weights
4 Starboard leading edge fuel tank, total internal
   capacity 341 Imp gal (410 US gal, 1552-lit)
5 Zero-length rocket installation (early P-38L)
6 Fuel filler cap
7 Aileron cable quadrant and hydraulic booster
8 Trim tab
9 Fixed tab
10 Starboard outboard Fowler-type flap segment

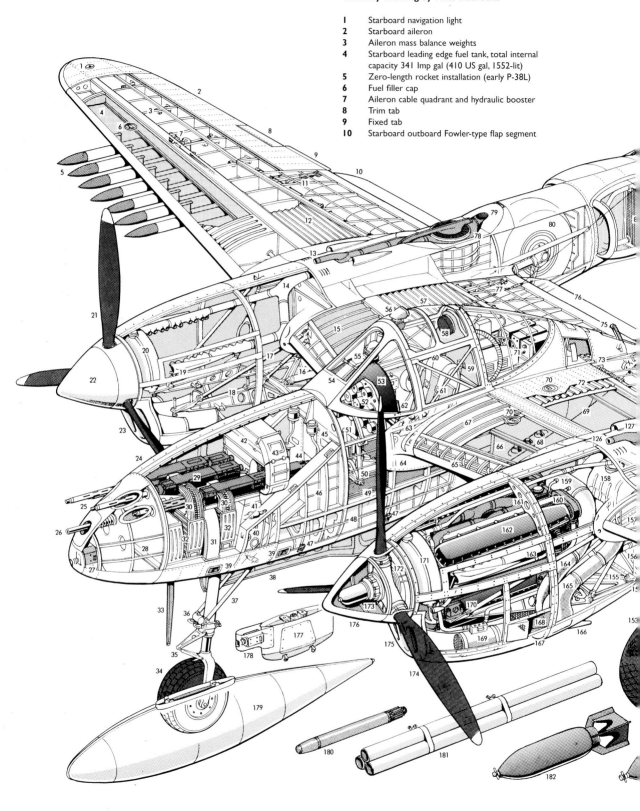

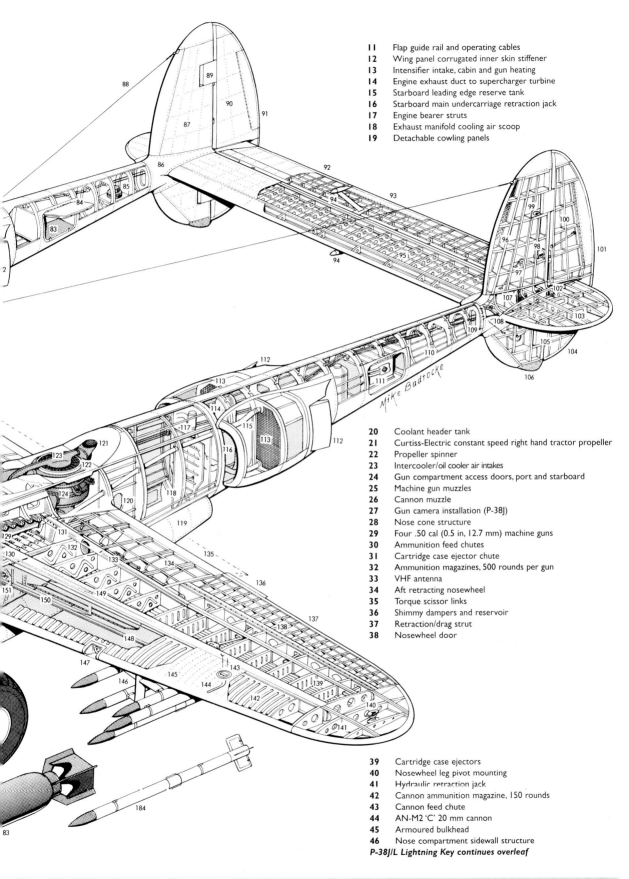

11 Flap guide rail and operating cables
12 Wing panel corrugated inner skin stiffener
13 Intensifier intake, cabin and gun heating
14 Engine exhaust duct to supercharger turbine
15 Starboard leading edge reserve tank
16 Starboard main undercarriage retraction jack
17 Engine bearer struts
18 Exhaust manifold cooling air scoop
19 Detachable cowling panels

Mike Badrocke

20 Coolant header tank
21 Curtiss-Electric constant speed right hand tractor propeller
22 Propeller spinner
23 Intercooler/oil cooler air intakes
24 Gun compartment access doors, port and starboard
25 Machine gun muzzles
26 Cannon muzzle
27 Gun camera installation (P-38J)
28 Nose cone structure
29 Four .50 cal (0.5 in, 12.7 mm) machine guns
30 Ammunition feed chutes
31 Cartridge case ejector chute
32 Ammunition magazines, 500 rounds per gun
33 VHF antenna
34 Aft retracting nosewheel
35 Torque scissor links
36 Shimmy dampers and reservoir
37 Retraction/drag strut
38 Nosewheel door

39 Cartridge case ejectors
40 Nosewheel leg pivot mounting
41 Hydraulic retraction jack
42 Cannon ammunition magazine, 150 rounds
43 Cannon feed chute
44 AN-M2 'C' 20 mm cannon
45 Armoured bulkhead
46 Nose compartment sidewall structure
P-38J/L Lightning Key continues overleaf

47 Rocket launcher attachment fittings (P-38J)
48 Underfloor nosewheel bay
49 Cockpit floor level
50 Rudder pedals
51 Control column, offset to starboard
52 Instrument panel
53 Instrument panel shroud
54 Armoured windscreen panel
55 Lynn-3 reflector sight
56 Rear view mirror
57 Rearward hingeing canopy upper segment
58 Headrest
59 Pilot's head armour
60 Roll-down side window panel
61 Pilot's armoured seat
62 Control column handwheel
63 Engine throttle and propeller control levers
64 Wing root fillet
65 Leading edge engine control runs
66 Port leading edge reserve tank
67 Chordwise tank bay stiffeners and inner skin panel
68 Ventral signal lights
69 Port inboard main fuel tank
70 Fuel filler caps
71 Radio equipment bay
72 Tank bay skin panel and spanwise corrugated inner stiffener
73 Flap drive motor and screw jack
74 Boarding step, extended
75 Step operating latch/grab handle
76 Starboard inboard Fowler-type flap segment
77 Flap outer guide rail and cable drive
78 Starboard supercharger
79 Exhaust gate
80 Starboard mainwheel, stowed position
81 Coolant radiators
82 Radiator exhaust flap
83 Stowage locker, tool kit and pilot's personal equipment
84 Hinged locker hatch
85 Master compass transmitter
86 Fin/tailplane root fairing
87 Starboard fin – fins interchangeable port and starboard
88 HF antenna cable
89 Rudder mass balance
90 Starboard rudder
91 Rudder trim tab
92 One-piece elevator
93 Elevator trim tab
94 Mass balance weights, upper and lower
95 Tailpane rib structure
96 Port fin structure
97 Elevator operating cable
98 Rudder trim actuator
99 Tail navigation light
100 Port rudder rib structure
101 Port rudder tab
102 Rudder hinge control
103 Fixed tailplane tip
104 Ventral rudder segment
105 Rudder mass balance
106 Tail bumper
107 Elevator control horn, cable
108 Rudder cable quadrant
109 Tailplane/tailboom attachment joint
110 Tailboom frame structure – booms interchangeable port and starboard
111 Battery compartment
112 Radiator exhaust flaps
113 Port engine coolant radiators, inner and outer
114 Oxygen bottle
115 Coolant pipes
116 Radiator fixed intake

117 Vertical flare launcher
118 Port main undercarriage wheel bay
119 Mainwheel door
120 Wheel bay and supercharger housing sidewall structure
121 Supercharger exhaust gate
122 Exhaust-driven turbine
123 Turbine and bearing cooling duct
124 Port intensifier intake
125 Engine exhaust duct to turbine drive
126 Port intensifier intake
127 Supercharger cooling air intakes
128 Outer wing panel main spar joint
129 Corrugated skin stiffener butt joints
130 Mainwheel leg bay-mounted supercharger intake air filter
131 Rear spar joint
132 Supercharger ram air intake
133 Flap push-pull control rod and operating cable drive
134 Flap shroud ribs
135 Port outboard Fowler-type flap
136 Aileron fixed tab
137 Port aileron
138 Aileron rib structure
139 Outer wing panel rib structure
140 Port navigation light
141 Wing tip structure
142 Leading edge tank bay inner corrugated skin stiffener
143 Tank filler cap
144 Ventral pitot head
145 Leading edge skin panel
146 Five-round cluster-type 'Christmas-tree' rocket launcher (late-model P-38L)
147 Landing light (P-38L)
148 Port leading edge fuel tank
149 Main spar booms and capping strip
150 Ventral dive flap, electrically-operated
151 Main undercarriage leg pivot mounting
152 Mainwheel leg strut
153 Port mainwheel, aft retracting
154 Retraction/drag strut
155 Engine bearer cast sub-frame
156 Engine bay firewall
157 Upper engine bearer support structure
158 Engine oil tank
159 Carburettor intake duct
160 Air-cooled magneto housings
161 Cowling support structure
162 Allison V-1710-89/91 (P-38J) or V-1710-111/113 (P-38L) V12 engine
163 Port exhaust manifold
164 Intercooler inlet duct to carburettor
165 Intercooler inlet duct
166 Cooling air exhaust flap
167 Ventral intercooler radiator
168 Oil cooler exhaust
169 Outboard oil cooler, twin coolers inboard and outboard
170 Forward engine mounting
171 Coolant header tank
172 Armoured spinner backplate
173 Propeller hub pitch change mechanism
174 Port Curtiss-Electric constant-speed left hand tractor propelle,
175 Oil cooler and intercooler air intakes
176 Port propeller spinner
177 Port wing pylon, mounted beneath inner wing panel
178 Gun camera installation (P-38L)
179 125 Imp gal (150-US gal, 568-lit) external tank
180 4.5-in (11.5-cm) M8 rocket projectile
181 M10 triple-tube 'Bazooka' rocket launcher, fuselage side mounted on P-38J
182 500-lb (227-kg) HE bomb
183 1000-lb (454-kg) HE bomb
184 4.5-in (11.5-cm) rocket